5-23-60

90-4374

50

Ancient Peoples and Places

BRITTANY

P. R. Giot
in collaboration with
J. L'Helgouach and J. Briard

73 PHOTOGRAPHS
48 LINE DRAWINGS
AND 20 MAPS

FREDERICK A. PRAEGER, *Publishers*
New York

THIS IS VOLUME THIRTEEN IN THE SERIES
Ancient Peoples and Places

GENERAL EDITOR: DR GLYN DANIEL

BOOKS THAT MATTER
Published in the United States of America
in 1960 by Frederick A. Praeger, Inc., Publishers
64 University Place, New York 3, N.Y.
All rights reserved
© Thames and Hudson, London, 1960
Library of Congress catalog card number 60-7378
Printed in Great Britain by Western Printing Services Ltd., Bristol

CONTENTS

ILLUSTRATIONS

Foreword

BRITTANY IS A LAND rich in prehistoric and protohistoric remains which has long attracted the attention of research workers and scholars. Numerous compilations, excavation reports and special treatises resulted, and these have often been of considerable value. But they were localised or regional, and dealt mainly with details. An overall synthesis has been long overdue. This, after twelve years of collecting the necessary material and data, the author has here sought to provide, with the able assistance of two of his students who in the process have become his close and trusted associates. Indeed, without their valuable individual contributions (J. Briard is responsible for Chapters VIII and IX; J. L'Helgouach for Chapters III and V; and both of them for Chapters IV and VI), this book would never have been completed.

Owing to the limitations imposed by the series of which it forms a part, it has not been possible in this volume to describe in detail the different cultures that succeeded each other in Brittany, or more exactly in Armorica, before the dawn of history. This would require a book of far ampler proportions. The author hopes, however, that the present work has succeeded in its more modest aim—to provide a conspectus of archaeological information on Brittany which will not only be of value to archaeologists and students, but will also awaken the interest of the layman in a region of France that has so much to offer the observant visitor.

The author and his collaborators wish to take this opportunity to thank all those persons who have so generously aided them in their work, from the members of their own staff and academic colleagues to the Keepers of Museums and of public

13

and private collections, and the officials of the Centre National de la Recherche Scientifique and the Direction Générale de l'Architecture, as well as correspondents and friends too numerous to mention by name.

P. R. G.

Note:

'Rivière d'Etel', 'rivière de Crach' and 'rivière d'Audierne' have been tendered as 'the Etel river', 'the Crach river' and 'the Audierne river' respectively, the Author having named these small rivers after the town situated where each flows into the sea. In all other instances the form 'the river Loire' or, simply, 'the Blavet' has been used.

The Country

THE PREHISTORIC PEOPLING of Brittany was governed at all periods by the same geographical and geological conditions and characteristics as it is today. There is, however, one important difference: since political 'frontiers' as we now know them did not exist, the region was often much more open to outside influences, instead of being shut in and isolated at the end of a remote peninsula. Brittany's chief 'natural frontier'—the sea, which borders two-thirds of its perimeter,—has indeed frequently served as a link, a means of access and penetration, once men had learned to navigate by coasting along the shores, or could venture upon the high seas. At many stages in its prehistory, Brittany was one of a group of Atlantic countries rather than an outlying dependency of Gaul. We shall constantly encounter a shifting of balance between the civilising influences from the continent and those filtering in through the English Channel (with the North Sea beyond), and the Atlantic, across the 'Celtic Sea' and via the Gulf of Gascony. Moreover, from the Iberian Peninsula to the British Isles there are lands made up of older rocks, such as Galicia and Cornwall, where conditions are very similar to those in Brittany.

Brittany is in fact part of the ancient Armorican *massif*, formed mainly of crystalline rocks and palaeozoic sediments, very consolidated or metamorphic (schists, quartzites), where calcareous deposits are rare. The absence of limestone accounts for the lack of caves, other than those due to marine erosion. Although relatively little mineralised, the ancient massif nevertheless contains appreciable lodes of tin, lead and iron, small and scattered amounts of silver and gold, and an

THE
SUBSOIL

insignificant quantity of copper. Dykes of hard intrusive rocks are plentiful.

Flint-bearing formations, particularly chalk, exist only in fairly remote mesozoic basins, and also in submarine deposits at some distance from the present-day shoreline (though seaweed and currents may of course have carried nodules to the offshore bars). In the Tertiary period, lateritic phenomena profoundly altered certain topographical surfaces, while in some places quartzites and silicifications were formed which served as replacement raw material during various prehistoric periods.

Finally, in the Pleistocene period, successive periglacial phenomena played an important part in Armorica, accumulating detritus on certain slopes and cliffs, and depositing coverings of loessic ooze, particularly on the Channel side. These phenomena have had an important influence on the living conditions of the earliest inhabitants.

THE RELIEF An old massif, but much levelled and eroded, and little chiselled by minor natural causes, Brittany cannot really be described as a highland region, since hardly any of it is more than 200 m. above sea-level. Only along a few rocky crests, or in the 'mountain' regions of the interior, rising to between 250 and 384 m., does the eye find relief from a harsh and desolate landscape in limitless panoramas, in contrast to the monotonous and peneplained horizons lying below. Such is the case, at least, on the relatively rare fine days; these hills easily trap the clouds and experience far more rainfall and overcast weather than the lowlands, as well as being as windy as the most exposed sea-shores.

THE SOIL The soils of Brittany can be classed as 'brown earths'; azonal, slightly podzolic soils providing excellent forest land in this oceanic climate. Owing to the lack of lime and phosphates, there is considerable acidity; bone objects, therefore, are not readily preserved. In most places, above the crystalline or palaeozoic subsoils, there is a grey surface soil; this between 10 and 20 cm. down has lost its colour through the leaching of the humus and the oxides, which are often carried down and form accumulations at a certain depth. Of course, where the coating of loess subsists on the Channel side, as also on the former muds and dunes along the shores, conditions are very different.

In general, in the interior of the country the layer of arable soil is shallow, and one soon reaches the underlying rocks, whether decayed or still relatively sound. As a result, conditions are unfavourable for the preservation by stratification of successive occupations, and the plough is constantly turning up, all mixed together, tools and other remains varying in date from the lower Palaeolithic era to the present day. It is only in large artificially accumulated structures that any depth is to be found; and ancient works involving cutting, such as trenching, are always on a small scale because of the difficulty in obtaining depth. Hence complete stratigraphical sequences are rare.

The Breton flora is essentially Atlantic in character; but the appearance of the vegetation covering the area today can give no idea of the natural plant formations that existed in the area in prehistoric and protohistoric times. No more than five or ten per cent is now covered with forest. The disappearance of the forest is disguised to some extent by the *Bocage* type of country (i.e. areas where hedgerows and copses are found), but this is only the result of cultivation. The poorest soils, or those most degraded by deforestation (and therefore acidified) have developed into moorland, where, since the nineteenth century, the introduction of pines has given a little variety to the skylines of heather, gorse and broom. But all this is secondary, and is the result of traditional agricultural exploitation based on rotation, fallow land and its subsequent clearance.

THE VEGETA-TION

We have little evidence from pollen-analysis, and what there is takes us scarcely farther back than the Neolithic period. Combined with geo-botanical data, and the comparison with regions where conditions are more or less similar, it enables us to form an approximate picture of the variations in plant life during the last millennia. The vegetation was mainly of broad-leaved trees, growing in summer and shedding their leaves in winter.

In the Mesolithic Age, during the pre-Boreal period, the climate was still dry and cold. Sea-level must still have been 15 to 20 m. lower than it is now, permitting the trees to advance farther along the coast. Birch and willow must have been plentiful (there is evidence of pine to the east of the Armorican *massif*, but as pine pollen is very easily carried by the wind, it may perhaps have come from the British Isles).

During the Boreal period, though the interior continued to experience a dry continental (xerothermic) climate, that of the Breton coast must have been more oceanic. The mixed oak forests and the maximum of hazel appear simultaneously, instead of following one another.

In pre-Neolithic times, during the Atlantic period, the climate was warm and damp; now the mixed oak forests reach their maximum extension, birch becomes rarer in the interior of the region, and the pine pollen, perhaps brought from a distance by the wind, gradually disappears. In the Neolithic Age itself, there was a big increase in the amount of alder adjoining the oak forests. Near peat bogs and around damp depressions alders must have been plentiful, though they were less numerous in windy situations such as the coastal area and the Yeun-Elez (the Monts d'Arrée peat bogs, where some fir-tree pollen has been found). On drier soil there were oak forests with under-growth and clearings of hazel. There must have been gaps in the forest; in less fertile zones there were heathlands, more or less peaty; near the coast elms were to be found among the oaks.

Finally, human intervention began the work of deforestation, by the system of cultivation on burnt clearings and the raising of sheep, cattle and pigs, which eat the young shoots.

In Late Neolithic and Chalcolithic times, and in the Bronze Age, during the sub-Boreal period, the climate became colder and drier, and this change corresponded with the second growth of hazel, and an increase of birch in the interior regions. There must at times have been heavy rainfall, because of the proximity of the sea. The sea-level, slowly rising since Palaeolithic times, gradually diminished the surface of land lying at the foot of the old cliffs, cutting off peninsulas into islands and rocks.

At the end of the Bronze Age and during the Iron Age, in the sub-Atlantic period, rain was more plentiful; beech and hornbeam, previously rare, appear in the east and in the interior of the region. The alder becomes less frequent, as the woods disappear in turn from the peat areas and their surroundings. There is an increase in the amount of beech growing in the interior, where birches also reappear. Oak replaces alder near the coast, where the rising sea-level begins to encroach seriously on the low-lying areas.

Finally, during the late sub-Atlantic period, in historic times, deforestation becomes general with the increase in agriculture and the spread of meadow and moorland. In the surviving areas of matured forest to the south, beech gains the upper hand, mingled with the common oak, while to the north and in the interior the robur-oak predominates. The latter does well in established forests, but in groves and copses it has in recent times been attacked by a fungus which gives it an unnatural stunted appearance. The sea-level seems to have reached its maximum height in the Dark Ages; not only does the sea flood, or re-cover during high tides, many prehistoric monuments or settlements that used to be situated by the shore, but also sand is blown up on to the mainland to form significant dunes, where a characteristic type of vegetation has taken root.

THE
FAUNA

The little we know about the game which was hunted indi-cates the existence of the usual mammals in the temperate forests. In the Mesolithic period there were beavers and wild cats; the last wolves were killed at the end of the nineteenth century, but there is no evidence of their presence during the later prehistoric periods. To judge by the frequency with which the remains of cetaceans are found in an archaeological context, they must often have been stranded on the shore. The great auk still existed in Mesolithic times.

CHAPTER II

The Beginnings of Man in Armorica

BRITTANY, A PENINSULA reaching out into the ocean, formed of pre-cambrian and palaeozoic rocks with exten- sive outcrops of crystalline ones, was more sparsely inhabited during the Old Stone Age than other regions of Gaul more fortunate in their plant and animal life and their climate, with plentiful supplies of flint and other stones that could be worked by flaking, and where caves and shelters were more frequent.

The majority of the Old Stone Age settlements which have been found in Armorica are near the coast. Probably much of the food was obtained from the sea, and it may also be that many deposits are now under water, as a result of the variations in the shore line during the Quaternary period. Other sites exist near outcrops of replacement rocks suitable for chipping, such as sandstone and quartzite.

Fig. 1

A full account of the Palaeolithic Age in Brittany would require lengthy incursions into geology, palaeontology and palaeo-climatology, which would be out of place here. We will therefore confine ourselves to an indication of the main features.

THE LOWER PALAEO- LITHIC AGE

Of the hundreds of thousands of years occupied by the earliest Lower Palaeolithic Age, little is known in Brittany either where its regional geology or its archaeology are concerned. A few chipped implements have been found—hand-axes all of an Acheulean type; in addition, more doubtful tools have been discovered, in a number of places.

Fig. 2

It is not until the last interglacial period, and the beginnings of the final glaciation, marked in Armorica by abundant peri- glacial deposits, that we find a more widespread peopling of the region, to which settlements with complex industries bear witness. Several surface chipping-floors are known, interesting

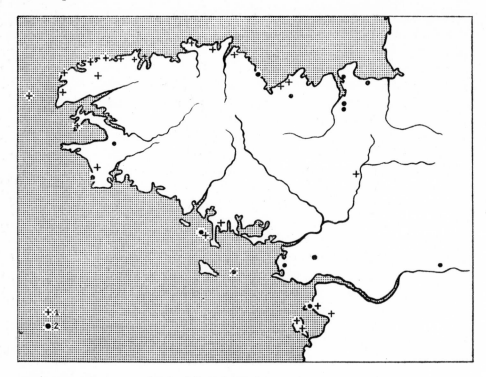

Fig. 1 Distribution map of Palaeolithic and Mesolithic: 1, isolated finds; 2, sites

only on account of the typology of the implements chipped from various kinds of quartzite (chipping-floors of Saint-Helen and Pleudihen; La Poterie, near Lamballe, Côtes-du-Nord; chipping-floor of Kervouster, Guengat, Finistère; sites at L'Ouchette and Pas-Chalène, Montbert; Pierre-Meslière-L'Etranglard, at Saint-Géréon, Loire-Atlantique). Usually the industry is Mousterian, but in the Acheulean tradition.

Only two important sites provide good stratigraphical evidence; both are at the bottom of the Norman-Breton gulf, in Ille-et-Vilaine. The recently discovered rock-shelter of Grainfollet, at Saint-Suliac, on the eastern bank of the Rance estuary,[1] is at the foot of a cliff and at the level of the present-day high tides, which had destroyed a great deal of it before it was excavated. There was a hearth there, set in clay almost on the rock itself, dating from the beginning of Würm I, with animal debris near it (*Elephas primigenius, Equus sp., Cervus sp.*). A flourishing flint industry existed, also using quartz and other rocks, together with rare Micoquian hand-axes, and especially flake-implements difficult to separate from Mousterian work in the Acheulean tradition. No doubt the industry was of a late and attenuated Micoquian character.

The classical Mont-Dol deposit was originally on the slope of a rocky islet in the middle of what were to become the Dol marshes; it occupied a sheltered position at the foot of a granite cliff, which perhaps actually overhung it at the beginning. The archaeological strata, mixed by solifluxian streams, may have shifted; they contained, together with ashes and calcined bones, products of a fairly classical Mousterian industry. There was

Fig. 2 Acheulean hand-axe of quartzite from the shore at Porspoder (F.). ¼

abundant variety of animals (*Elephas primigenius, Rhinoceros antiquitatis, Equus caballus, Cervus megaceros, Rangifer tarandus, Bos primigenius, Canis lupus, Ursus spelaeus, Arctomys marmotta*), also dating from Würm times.

THE UPPER PALAEOLITHIC AGE In Brittany proper there is no settlement which can be ascribed with certainty to the full Upper Palaeolithic period. It is not till one reaches the eastern edge of the Armorican massif that one finds well stratified caves (Mayenne) or a few surface sites (late ones, moreover) to the south of the Loire (Bégrolles).[2] The lack of almost all calcareous rock, and therefore of caves, seems to be the chief reason for this gap. Along the Channel shores, a few isolated flint implements found in the most recent loessic silt have sometimes been attributed to this period.

In Finistère, on the other hand, a site going back to the Epipalaeolithic (or extreme Upper Palaeolithic) period was excavated a long time ago: the cave of Roc'hToul, Guiclan.[3] An openair site adjoins it. This cave is situated in a ridge of metamorphic quartzite, thanks to faults in the rock—a detail which shows how much the absence of caves handicapped the inhabitants of the region at this period. The industry discovered on this site has recently been compared with the Arudian products from the Pyrenees; it is very rough work, and mostly of local quartz.

THE MESOLITHIC PERIOD The most important Mesolithic sites in Brittany are situated on islands and on a peninsula, all of which at that period were certainly joined to the mainland. These are the only certain and pure Mesolithic remains, and are no doubt relatively late, dating from an epoch when the first Neolithic cultures were already flourishing in southern parts of Gaul.

The type site is that of Téviec (or Tiviec), SaintPierre Quiberon (Morbihan),[4] a rocky islet to the west of the Quiberon peninsula. On a part of the coast facing northwest the exposed archaeological layer, in the form of blackish carbonaceous earth full of the remains of edible shellfish, and up to about a metre thick, occupied an area of about 200 sq. m. In this mass of kitchen refuse numerous domestic hearths, seven large ritual hearths, and ten graves containing the remains of twenty-three skeletons were found. The layer was perfectly homogeneous, both as regards the period of culture and the fauna, and was completely undisturbed.

A second site is that of Hoëdic (Morbihan),[5] last of the chain of islets enclosing the bay of Quiberon. On the eastern side of a headland situated in the north-west of the island, the archaeo-logical layer, covered by a dune containing late Neolithic material at its base, occupied 200 sq. m.; it took the form of kitchen debris as in the other site, but was only 30 to 40 cm. deep. The domestic hearths are scarcely distinguishable from one another, and the site included nine graves containing thirteen skeletons.

A third site is that of the Torche peninsula in Plomeur (Finistère; Beg-an-Dorchenn),[6] in the bay of Audierne, which originally extended for several hundred square metres, and was about one metre thick, with shallower extensions. At least three domestic hearths have been identified successively in the last strip left untouched by marine erosion, but no graves of the period have been found. Late Neolithic and Iron Age layers directly superimposed, and sometimes involving disturbance and digging, have complicated the task of observation.

All this refuse indicates a poor standard of feeding, most of the nourishment being obtained from the sea, particularly in the form of shellfish (collected most easily, and with least danger); hardly any fish, except at La Torche; very few traces of game—boar, stag, goat, and even more rarely, other animals. At Téviec, carbonised wild pears were found, and the bones of a dog (no doubt domesticated). There is very little evidence of any stone or bone industry among the debris.

The Téviec and Hoëdic sites are particularly interesting on account of their cemeteries, scattered amongst the remains of the settlement without any definite orientation, the graves being half sunk into the subsoil and half buried in the kitchen refuse, which at Téviec covered them in every case. Thanks to

Plate 1

the extremely skilful excavations of the discoverers of these sites, they have yielded up two series of skeletons of particular importance for the study of Mesolithic anthropology and the funerary rites of the period.

The cemetery at Téviec consisted of ten graves, containing the remains of twenty-three bodies; the tombs, therefore, each contained from one to six persons, of all ages and both sexes. The cemetery at Hoëdic consisted of nine tombs containing fourteen individuals, from one to three in each tomb. These multiple inhumations are 'family vaults', with successive burials and double inhumations—often an adult with a child in its arms. The bodies must have been tied up with the legs forced back behind the loins. They have been lightly sprinkled with ochre. A ritual hearth was usually established above the graves, and at Téviec in particular actual stone mausoleums were erected over them. Some of the graves of adults contained antler furnishings; but whereas at Téviec the corpse was framed in antlers, at Hoëdic it was surrounded with both antlers and antler tools.

The funerary furnishings include flint implements and, in particular, bone daggers as well as ornaments made of sea shells, pierced and strung into necklaces, bracelets and anklets. Some of the objects bear a few engraved lines.

To judge from their stone industry—which, in addition to miscellaneous pebble tools and flints only slightly trimmed, also included microlithic implements of geometric form, scalene triangles, trapezoids and blades with retouched oblique cutting—these settlements are related to a pure Tardenoisian culture, considered sometimes to be a coastal or littoral form, or a marginal aspect.

A number of surface sites with what appears to be a Tardenoisian industry near the eastern limits of Brittany seem in fact to contain Neolithic elements, according to information so far available.

CHAPTER III

The First Neolithic Cultures of Armorica

AFTER THE FINAL GLACIATION, the climate of south-western Asia and of most of Europe gradually became milder, and it was then that an extremely important cultural revolution took place in the more favoured regions, which opened the way for new cultures. This revolution was marked by a complete change in the economy of prehistoric peoples. Abandoning his destructive way of life, based solely on the exploitation of natural resources, with all the uncertainty which that involved, Man succeeded in making himself master of his means of food production. He recognised the nourishment value of certain wild cereals; he learnt to sow and harvest them, and little by little he evolved new varieties. In the same way, he domesticated certain animals. This advance brought in its train the formation of larger social organisations, grouped around cattle enclosures and cultivated fields, and henceforth protected by new divinities.

However, the Armorican region was still in the Mesolithic stage of development, and remained so for some time, while the Neolithic way of life typical of the New Stone Age was flourishing in the Near East and later in other parts of the Mediterranean. In fact, though certain waves from the expanding Neolithic culture flowed towards the West from the Fertile Crescent of the Near East, it was only the final ripples of the last of these waves that reached the shores of Armorica.

The Neolithic influences arriving by the Danubian route, which travelled down the Rhine valley and reached the river mouth before 4000 B.C.,[1] later spreading into the Paris basin, filtered into Normandy and Jersey (e.g. the lower layer of the Pinnacle settlement,[2] with perforated dolerite hammers and

curiously decorated pottery), without giving any definite indications of their presence in Brittany.

Along the Mediterranean route, there were several instances
of the expansion of Neolithic civilisation, the earliest of which
scarcely extended beyond the shores of the western Mediterranean. The later ones reached the whole of western Europe,
affecting various regions in different ways. Together, these make
up a group of Neolithic cultures characterised by a family of
pottery known as 'western', of which the earliest dated examples,
which come from Brittany, at present go back to about 3140 B.C.
(so that one would expect these cultures to have begun around
3500 B.C.).

Armorica was therefore soon influenced by this stage of Neolithic culture. Late Neolithic culture is still much more abundant, including even a quantity of very belated Neolithic material;
its industry shows new forms, but continues to use older types
(older Neolithic forms of pottery being made with a change of
paste). Superimposed on these two main phases of Neolithic cultures, and more or less coeval with at least part of both of them,
an Armorican Chalcolithic culture is represented by the diffusion
of Beaker pottery, and the first metal objects associated with it.

In regions of Western Europe where natural caves existed,
these served as tombs for Neolithic Man; elsewhere, if the rock
was soft enough, artificial caves were dug. Perhaps this
suggested the idea of erecting on flat ground buildings which
resembled small caverns when covered with a mound of earth
or a cairn of stones. As these monuments were usually built
with big slabs of stone, this type of architecture is known as
'megalithic'.

Monuments which appear alike, but which actually belong
to very different epochs, exist all over the world. Even in
Europe the various groups of megalithic tombs are not
definitely related to one another, nor had they all a common
source. The idea may have originated in the eastern Mediter-

ranean about the early fourth millennium B.C., and spread to the western Mediterranean towards the end of the same millennium; the true megalithic cultures of western Europe probably derived from this source.

The Passage Graves form a first group; in Brittany they are called *dolmens*, from an eighteenth-century composition of the Breton words *taol* and *maen*—table of stone (but in the eleventh century the word 'tolmaen' is attested in a cartulary). Basically, they consist of a chamber with a corridor leading into it; they are enclosed in circular mounds or cairns, often very large. The immediate prototypes of these are found throughout the south and west of Iberia, together with rock-cut tombs of the same plan. This type of building subsequently spread to Armorica early in the heyday of the western Neolithic cultures.

The second group consists of the **Gallery Graves** (in French: *allées couvertes*). These are long monuments which may or may not be divided into compartments, and are enclosed in a long mound which does not necessarily cover them. Prototypes of these monuments are to be found in different parts of southern Gaul, from which they may have reached Brittany and the Paris basin by way of the west-central region, at the moment when the Late Neolithic cultures were established.

Such schematic derivations are in fact no more than simplifications. A great many monuments, generally late in date, cannot be easily fitted into the artificial framework of a rigid typology, and were perhaps built on very rudimentary lines.

In Armorica, the influence of megalithic culture was soon very strong; this can be discerned from the way the low Neolithic mounds were constructed, though they proceeded from a more archaic tradition, because already some megalith-builders had appeared on the scene. And much later, in the Bronze Age, the practices of the last megalith-builders left their mark on the construction of the internal chambers of the barrows.

It is impossible as yet to demonstrate the Neolithic cultures of Brittany, in the broad sense, in a purely chronological way; nor is it possible, moreover, to use a purely cultural point of view. Roughly, the western Neolithic culture gives way to a later Neolithic culture, with some overlapping and inter-mixture.[3] The first appearance of metal, in the form of a sort of diffuse Chalcolithic culture, is interwoven with the end of the primordial western Neolithic, and the beginning of the Late Neolithic culture, showing that chronologically the last-named is a very belated Neolithic, especially as communities belonging to it seem to have gone on with their rather antiquated mode of life right on into the Bronze Age. For convenience' sake we shall distribute the information in three chapters, this one dealing with the real Neolithic, the next with the elements of a Chalcolithic culture which flourished just prior to the inci-dence of the later Neolithic, and a third chapter with the later and belated Neolithic culture itself. Such a distribution would seem, on the whole, to give a reasonably balanced picture, and one that allows for the diverse factors, while not pretending to be anything like a chronological sequence.

NEOLITHIC
POTTERY

The pottery ascribed to the true Neolithic culture, of Western affinities, in Brittany, although it provides the earliest examples of ceramics in Breton prehistory, already shows an advanced stage of development. We possess, of course, pots and fragments of pots which can very well be compared with the pottery of the Cortaillod and Chassey cultures, and—more remotely—with certain features of the Almerian, Lagozza, Windmill Hill or even Michelsberg cultures. In fact, however, this Armorican pottery has always a direct or indirect connexion with the megalithic religion. Thus it is risky to describe material of the Neolithic culture in Brittany as being of the Chassey type. Because of this connexion, Breton pottery, finally influenced by the new techniques of the Late Neolithic, is another local aspect of western Neolithic pottery, and is not often found in a pure form.

The ware is thin, generally 6 to 8 mm. thick (some very small vessels are only 3 to 4 mm. thick), and well-fired, which makes it homogeneous; one never finds inner variations due to defective firing. The outside colour varies from fairly pale beige to a rich black; the exterior is burnished and specks of mica sparkle on its surface; there is never any calcitic *dégraissant*, as in other regions.

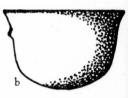

The forms are simple. Typically, the base of the vessel is rounded, and the body spherical (the so-called apodal vessels). The shape of the pots, and the thinness and lustre of the best ware, recall imitations of leather vessels. Perhaps the most usual shape is a kind of spherical bowl 7 to 10 cm. high, with a maximum width of 10 to 15 cm. There are many variations; the edge can be straight or curved; in the latter case a pronounced rolling may produce an S-shaped profile. In the case of straight edges, the rim is sometimes fairly tall; there is then a definite demarcation between the body of the vessel and its neck, which is cylindrical. This gives it the appearance of a round-based bottle.

Fig. 3 Neolithic pots: a, with perforated vertical lug, from the Passage Grave of Park-Néhué, Riantec (M.); b, with button lug, from the Passage Grave of Lann-Kerber, Belz (M.). Both ¼

However, there is not always a clear division between the body and the neck; the vase is in this case pear-shaped, and its contour is not always regular. One should not overlook the relatively large numbers of very small vessels (2½ cm. to 5 cm. high) that are to be found in the shapes already described. Did such pigmy vessels serve some useful purpose? Were they employed in the making of plant decoctions or perfumes? It may be that they were simply offerings to the dead, or were used as playthings.

Not all these pots are provided with any sort of lug or means of suspension. Lugs, where they exist, are small, pinched in the thickness of the clay, in the form of a kind of knob. A means of suspension is provided by piercing holes in the vessel,

Figs. 3, 4

horizontally or vertically; the perforation is usually 'subcuta-neous', in the thickness of the body of the pot, and there is only a slight bulge at this point. Sometimes, however, there may be a considerable protuberance, through which the hole is made. Each vessel may have one or two lugs.

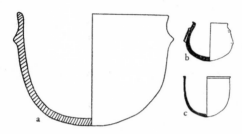

Fig. 4 Neolithic pots: a, with lugs from the buttressed Gallery Grave of Lesconil, Poullan (F.); b, with perforated vertical lug from the Passage Grave of Voguer-Men, Plogoff (F.); c, from the passage of Passage Grave H in the great cairn of Barnenez, Plouézoc'h (F.). All ¼

Most sites and monuments attributed to the true Neolithic culture (mounds, cists, simple Passage Graves) have provided examples of these types of pottery. Unfortunately, undamaged specimens are rare; the pottery is usually found in a frag-mentary state—broken pieces making up only small portions of several vessels.

Decoration is not often found on true Neolithic pottery. A quantity of decorated pottery which was included in the Chassey complex by some authors must in fact be ascribed to a later period as a result of our recent investigations. Its decoration may show some analogies with that of genuine Neolithic pottery, but the paste shows that it has come under influences from the late Neolithic, and is thus itself fairly late in date. We therefore have to eliminate most of the 'channelled' decora-tion,[4] especially of the type found on the round-bottomed pots of Conguel, Saint-Pierre-Quiberon (Morbihan), which is not so much true channelling as incisions made in a very thick clay. Indeed, genuine 'channelled ware' is rare in Brittany; it is marked with shallow lines traced in the unbaked clay with a blunt-ended object—a straw, or perhaps a finger-nail. The designs built up with these channellings are usually composed of halves of circles or ovals, arranged below the rim or on either side of double oblique lines, as on the fragments found in the mounds of Castellic and Mané-Hui, Carnac (Morbihan).

Plate 2

Although most of the pots with incised decoration belong to the Late Neolithic cultures, there are some which can be ascribed to the true Neolithic; but these are fairly rare. A few examples of decoration with triangles and squares with hatched grounds can probably be included in this category. The little pot from the Passage Grave of Er-Mar, Crach (Morbihan), decorated with 'horseshoes' finely patterned with squares, definitely belongs to the true Neolithic, and so does a little pot of identical shape and paste, found in the Passage Grave of Park-Néhué, Riantec (Morbihan). The latter is decorated with double scallops; a few fragments from the lower level of Passage Grave D in the cairn of Barnenez, Plouézoc'h (Finistère), carry exactly the same motif. The scallops and fern-leaves on the large pot from the Passage Grave of Penker-Bloa, Plomeur (Finistère), are fairly close to the latter, but they are executed in relief.

Plate 3

Plate 4

Probably related to the incised fragments from the Neolithic level of the Pinnacle site at Jersey, is a tiny fragment found in a mound at Saint-Just (Ille-et-Vilaine), which shows decoration carried out in a stab-and-drag technique, by pushing a twig into the clay and then drawing it downwards.

Although it is late in the south of Gaul, a decoration in relief in the form of little pimples is in Armorica contemporary with the Neolithic pottery (it is, moreover, found at this level at the Pinnacle in Jersey). These little protuberances are produced from the inside of the pot with a little twig, thus forming a bulge on the outside; the inner scar is then filled in. Fragments decorated in this way have been found on sites in Morbihan and Finistère, inside mounds in Morbihan and Ille-et-Vilaine, and in Passage Graves in Morbihan.

With regard to stone objects, we are even more handicapped than in the case of pottery by the absence of stratigraphy. In fact, a great many tools and weapons are found both in genuine Neolithic and in Late Neolithic cultures; it is therefore diffi´cult, in monuments where elements from both cultures are found together, to state exactly to which individual objects belong.

Amongst the flint objects, transverse arrow´heads are common. They are usually trapezoid (long or short) in shape, sometimes scalene, rarely triangular; they are cut from blades, and have one or two dorsal spines. The retouching ends abruptly; this differentiates them from the transverse arrows of the typical Chassey culture where the trimming extends in´wards. This may be due to a fairly strong persistence of Mesolithic traditions (the transverse arrows of the Neolithic level at the Pinnacle in Jersey are also steeply trimmed).

Leaf´shaped arrow´heads are exceptional in Armorica, at all periods. Tanged arrow´heads present more delicate prob´lems, as regards their typological evolution. The earliest are probably those that are very thick, with a very broad tang; their length may exceed their width, or both dimensions may be about the same. There are no barbs, so that the stem is either clearly differentiated or else merges imperceptibly into the head of the arrow, which in this case is almost lozenge´shaped.

It is not impossible that tanged and barbed arrow´heads may date from the true Neolithic culture. Unfortunately, the Passage Graves in which they have been found (Kercadoret, Locmaria´quer; Rogarte, Carnac, for example) also contained important Chalcolithic grave´goods; it is not impossible, therefore, that these splendid arrow´heads are not more closely allied to the Beaker, than to the fine Neolithic, pottery. The same situation is found in the lower layer of the chamber of Passage Grave D in the cairn of Barnenez, where a superb tanged and barbed arrow´head, similar to the lozenge´shaped arrow´heads of the

Early Bronze Age, was found near both Neolithic and Beaker pottery. Probably only a very complete study of western Neolithic arrow-heads would solve the problem.

The other flint objects, such as scrapers, awls, fabricators or blades, do not seem to show any typological evolution. They are very plentiful, but much less so than in regions where the raw material is easily available. The blades vary in size, and are sometimes fairly large; occasionally they are trimmed along the sides to produce a saw edge. The scrapers are disc-shaped, gibbous, or on the ends of blades.

Earlier authors wished to characterise the Neolithic Age by the polishing of stone. Although most of the polished axes of Brittany seem to date from the time of the Late Neolithic culture (and we will go into the problem of axes when discussing that culture), there is no doubt that a few of them are found in the true Neolithic. There are none in the low mounds in the interior, but they exist in those in the neighbourhood of Carnac, and in various small megalithic tombs. It should be observed that a certain number of these early axes are made of dolerite of the type we shall distinguish later as group A, showing that this rock was already in use.

Finally, of course, one finds everywhere a great quantity of pebbles used as makeshift tools—as strikers, retouching implements or fabricators, crushing tools, burnishers, grinding-stones and pestles.

Knowledge about the dwelling places of these populations is very scarce, because of unfavourable conditions.

OCCUPA-TION SITES

Nevertheless, an old occupation level is noticeable in different places of Leon district (northern Finistère) on the top of the loessic soil where this has been subsequently covered by a sand-dune, or as at Curnic, Guisseny, where it supported a sublittoral marsh-bog, now submerged by the raised sea-level. In it have been found flints, sherds of pottery and other implements, and numerous traces of fire: charcoal or burnt stones. In the same way, under the sands of the Quiberon isthmus, traces of hearths with scraps of industry of the same types have been noted here and there.

The Curnic site is the most important. In it have been dis-covered polished stone axes of fibrolite and dolerite of group A, including already a specimen of the button-axes. This site has been dated by the radio-carbon method to 3140 ±60 B.C., a fact that shows that the Neolithic culture of Brittany began well before 3000 B.C., as in most other parts of Western Europe.

THE LONG
MOUNDS

These monuments, whose purpose is definitely funerary, are not very numerous, and in Brittany are distributed in the interior and along the southern coasts. They actually constitute two parallel series, differing from one another in detail.

The long mounds of the interior: At Saint-Just, in the southern part of Ille-et-Vilaine, and at Le Quillio, in the southern part of Côtes-du-Nord, on high ground in areas which are still almost uncultivated, there exist several strange monuments.[5]

At Saint-Just there is a little series of them on a ridge of schist, the Grée-de-Cojoux—a vast moor with shallow soil. The best preserved is that of Croix-Saint-Pierre. It has two parallel rows of slabs, leaning outwards, running more or less in an east-west direction, but incomplete and overturned in parts. Old plans seem to show that the enclosure was in fact rectangular. To the west is a standing menhir just over 1 m. high. The stones of the south row are massive quartz blocks, while those of the north row are of schist and much thinner, creating a kind of asymmetry very characteristic of this type of monument. The rectangle is about 20 m. long, and a little more than 5 m. wide between the two rows of monoliths; the total width of the mound must be about 15 m. Its height, somewhat reduced by the action of water, is about 1 m. towards the centre. The funerary zone seems to have its centre of gravity at a large slab lying flat in the eastern part of the mound. The tomb must have been below it or around it, surrounded by a broken line of little stones, of charred wood and burnt earth. Around this slab was also found the funerary equipment—a fairly meagre collection, since it consisted only of flint flakes and a few little fragments of pottery.

This monument is associated, on the moors of Cojoux, with a large group of megalithic remains which includes, as well as other long mounds of similar construction, a Gallery Grave, semicircles and lines of menhirs, and a strange barrow, the Château-Bû, with some large menhirs and a few small vertical slabs upon it, which might well be a circular mound unique of its kind.

The long mound of Notre-Dame-de-Lorette at Le Quillio, on the other hand, is isolated from any other prehistoric traces on a heath 298 m. above sea-level, on a quartzite substratum covered with a thick layer of podzol. The structural charac-teristics are similar to those of the preceding example. The two rows of stones, leaning outwards, orientated east-west, outline an 'enclosure' 20 m. long and 7 m. wide. At each end of the two rows is a slab placed at right angles, marking the beginning of the short sides of the rectangle. The asymmetry of the two rows of stones is again very decided; those on the north are squat quartz blocks, those on the south are of schist, and much taller. Standing in the axis of the monument, 3 m. to the west, is a menhir 2 m. high. The whole construction has become considerably flatter in our own time. Only the eastern part, corresponding with the burial area, has produced a few objects —some tools of quartzite and fragments of pottery insignificant both in size and quantity.

Although the grave-goods found in these two long mounds are not very plentiful, they are nevertheless of interest because they make possible a comparison with other Breton graves. At Saint-Just, the stone objects consist of about forty flint implements, hardly any of which are typical; only three small blades show some retouching. At Le Quillio, on the other hand, out of five objects of quartzite, two are blades with no retouching, the other three are triangular edged arrows with steep trimming.

The pottery is all in fragments, and it is impossible to reconstruct its forms. It seems to be of a late western type, especially at Le Quillio, where some fragments show the beginning of a flat base. All the pieces found there, and most of those from the mound at SaintJust, are undecorated. Four pieces of the rims of pots from the latter monument are decorated; one has short incisions made when the clay was wet, no doubt with a straw, in stabanddrag technique; the three others have either one or two rows of pimples in relief. It should be noted that a few fragments found in association with a piece of a rough schist arcpendant, on the surface, appear definitely to belong to the Late Neolithic culture.

The coastal areas: In the Carnac region, there are fairly numerous long mounds, more or less intact according to the degree of investigation or local cultivation.[6] It is rather remarkable to find such a concentration of them in this region of megalithic tombs, but their relationship with the megaliths is not very clear.

Like the long mounds found in the interior, they almost always lie in a more or less eastwest direction. The mound of ManéTyEc at Crucuny, Carnac, however, is orientated northnortheast/southsouthwest. These monuments are not very high (1 to 2 m.), but they are very long. The longest seems to be that at Kerlescan (nearly 100 m.); the average length is about 40 to 50 m. The width varies from 15 to 35 m. It should also be noted that the eastern end is often the widest part. Unlike the inland long mounds, where the kerbstones often project from the summit of the barrow, the structures here are internal, entirely covered by the cairn, if it is intact. Moreover, the roughly rectangular enclosures consist only of little walls of dry stone, or a juxtaposition of small blocks. The material assembled for building the mound is usually a mixture of fairly large stones and earth.

However, the most important feature of the coastal long mounds, which distinguishes them from the others, is the presence of cists, in varying numbers, dispersed throughout the whole mound. At Kerlescan there are only five cists; at Manio they are far more numerous—over thirty have been counted. They are often built with four stones arranged on edge; they are about 10 cm. deep and their area is between 30 by 12 cm. and 40 by 20 cm. Each cist is surrounded by flat stones, corbelled out and covering it over. Sometimes they are more simply constructed, the stones surrounding them being propped against each other; such are to be found in the Castellic mound, next to circular cists.

Among the Carnac long mounds, that of Kerlescan is the only one marked by a small menhir to the west, as found with the inland mounds. There is also, nevertheless, a menhir $4\frac{1}{2}$ m. high at Manio, but this is at the eastern end of the monument, near a big slab covering a trench surrounded by coarse walling. The slab bears a representation of an axe with a handle; on the menhir are five wavy lines, usually identified as serpents. Five polished stone axes have been discovered at the base of this menhir. Was this perhaps the most important grave in the mound? It may very well be so, and may correspond with the position of the single tomb in the Saint-Just mounds, where at Croix-Saint-Pierre a large flat stone occurs at this point.

The long mounds at Carnac have yielded a fair amount of material, but mostly in a fragmentary state; it was found in the cists, around the hearths and in the heaped-up earth. Not all of the cists contained grave-goods; some were merely filled with black earth and carbonised wood.

Stone objects include flint implements (blades, points, scrapers, and transverse arrow-heads), polished stone axes (those found at the foot of the Manio menhir are of dolerite; at

Castellic and Kerlescan some are of fibrolite). At Manio, at the base of the menhir, there was too a quartz pendant, with a biconical perforation. We may mention also tools such as hammer-stones, querns and polishers.

As regards pottery, we have more information than for the inland monuments. Indeed, the mounds of Manio, Castellic and Kerlescan in particular have yielded a fairly considerable number of pots or large fragments. On the whole, the ware seems to be related to true western types. There are several round-bottomed forms, bowl-shaped or pear-shaped; sometimes they have a small neck, and lugs in the shape of a knob, the latter occasionally pierced horizontally. However, the ware is not always very fine, and some vessels are probably fairly late. For this reason, as well as because of its shape, a flat-based pot found at Manio seems to belong to the Late Neolithic culture. Also, two pots found at Kerlescan (on the summit of the cairn, it is true) are flat-based and thick, one being decorated with incised and dotted triangles, the other with a row of finger-pinchings round the body. In addition, at Castellic and Mané-Hui, Carnac, there have been found fragments of rims with pimples in relief decoration, alongside pieces of channelled ware typical of the true Neolithic culture, but in the large cist of Mané-Hui they were found in association with very highly evolved axes of jadeite and fibrolite, characteristic of the Carnac group of the Late Neolithic culture.

To the north-east of Guérande, at Bretineau near Bogat (Loire-Atlantique), is a monument which is probably also a long mound. The measurements of its trapezoidal enclosure correspond with those of the Carnac mounds (70 m. long and 8 to 12 m. wide); however, the kerb is formed by very large slabs 1·60 to 2·30 m. high, carefully aligned and almost touching, as in the inland mounds. Early excavations in this mound have revealed hearths distributed along an axial line and covered with blocks of stone. In the ashes of these hearths were found some bones, fragments of pottery (one decorated), and flint and quartz tools. Polished axes, three of dolerite, were found in the vicinity. The main axis of this mound lies more or less south-west/north-east, which is somewhat unusual.

Comparisons: There is no doubt about the relationship between the two series of funerary long mounds; both clearly derive from the same tradition. The principle of the kerb, the presence of menhirs indicating the site, the orientation, are the same in both groups. The important difference is in the number of graves contained in the mounds; where the inland mounds have a single grave, those of the Carnac group have clearly separated cists and hearths. In fact, the inland Breton mounds are closest to the English unchambered long barrows of the Windmill Hill culture. But the latter are usually built in chalk regions, and the enclosures were wooden posts of which traces have been found; these barrows generally have a single tomb at the east end. Similar monuments probably existed in the Paris basin, but intensive cultivation has levelled them all completely. But more or less related unchambered long barrows exist in the northern area, in northern Germany and in Poland, and we can expect the Breton mounds to be the ultimate version of a northern European family of tombs.

Unchambered long barrows belong to non-megalithic Neolithic cultures, and this is one of the chief reasons for ascribing the Breton long mounds to the true Neolithic culture. However, the objects found in them are not all very convincing, and except perhaps for a few typically western pots from the Carnac region, some of the pottery seems to be of a late date. This fact suggests that, in Brittany, these monuments are not necessarily earlier than the Passage Graves; they simply leave proof of a different tradition.

It should be noted that the Manio mound at Carnac is earlier than the Kermario alignments, which pass over it; and that, in the same way, the Kerlescan long mound is partly

covered by the semicircle of menhirs of the Kerlescan alignments. But this gives no very exact indication of age.

THE
PASSAGE
GRAVES

The main difficulty encountered in studying the Passage
Graves is the absence of any stratigraphy that might help to
establish the period in which they were constructed, and the
periods in which they were subsequently re-utilised. Most of
them were in fact in use for a very long time, and often contain
a large quantity of objects from the Late Neolithic cultures,
mixed with older true Neolithic material. Some Passage
Graves, however, have only produced Neolithic objects. In any
case, since all contain elements of early western Neolithic
culture, it must be admitted that nearly all simple Passage
Graves—all, that is, except the more evolved types, angled or
with lateral chambers—appeared at as early a date as that
given for the true Neolithic culture, coming from the South.
It is not impossible that many of the megalith builders came by
sea, along the western shores of Gaul. In any case, it is certain
that they sailed along the coast of Armorica; a study of the
distribution of simple Passage Graves is conclusive upon this
point—all are practically on the coast.

Fig. 5

Their maximum concentration is in the region of
Locmariaquer, Carnac and Quiberon, between the gulf of
Morbihan and the Etel river. There were more than a hundred
Passage Graves there, indicating a considerable density of
population.[7] No doubt, amongst the earliest arrivals there were
many who did not wish to travel further; a certain proli-
feration resulted, and this may explain why this region also
possesses many more advanced types of megalithic tombs.

In the same way, some tribes must have landed in the
estuaries of the Loire and the Vilaine, travelling for some
distance up the latter river and its tributaries.

Towards the west, the Passage Graves again provide us with
traces of the movement of these populations. They are spread

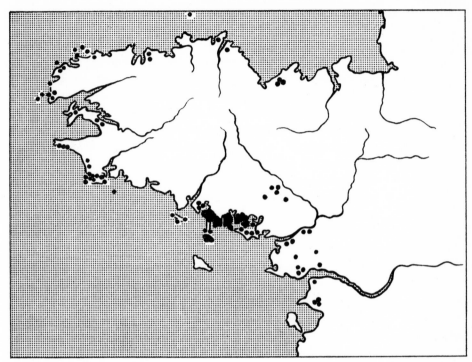

Fig. 5 Distribution map of Passage Graves

along the coastal areas, between the Etel river and the Blavet, in
the neighbourhood of Plouhinec, then between the Blavet and
the Laïta, near Ploemeur (Morbihan). Between the Laïta and
the Odet they are less thickly distributed, although still continuous. Passage Graves are also found on the islands of Groix
and Les Glénans, near the coast. In the Bigouden area itself, at
the western extremity of south Finistère, Passage Graves occur
in significant numbers. Those of the simple type are few, which
may indicate that the original settlers were not numerous, but
that there was a fairly rapid increase in population in this area—
the terminus of direct contact with the Morbihan regions.

Continuing their travels, the megalithic peoples colonised the west and north coasts of Armorica, but in a more scattered fashion. An exception is the Crozon peninsula, which contains a considerable number of more or less dilapidated simple Passage Graves. After that point, there is a continuous sprinkling of these graves along the banks of Léon and on the neighbouring islands—especially in the Molène archipelago.

Beyond the estuary at Morlaix, the Passage Graves thin out. Nevertheless, it is here that we find the two large cairns of Barnenez, Plouézoc'h dominating the estuary of the river, and one of which contains no less than eleven Passage Graves set side by side. After the graves of the Sept-Iles, of Kerbors, Yvias and Pléneuf (Côtes-du-Nord), one has to go as far as the Channel Islands and Calvados in order to meet Passage Graves again.

The position of Passage Graves in relation to the topography is constant. They are very rarely found in a depression or by the water; they are always on crests, hills or high ground. Even in areas where there is very little variation in level they are placed where they can at least slightly dominate their surroundings.

Plate 8
Plate 9

A Passage Grave comprises a passage leading to a clearly defined chamber. Such graves are best divided into two types, according to whether the passage is short or long. Of course, there are many intermediate stages between those with the shortest passages (which may be only 1 m. long) and those where the passage may be as much as 10 m. long, as at Barnenez, Plouézoc'h or even 14 m. as at Gavrinis, Larmor-Baden (Morbihan). The symmetry of the monuments depends on how the chamber is joined to the passage; if both have the same axis the megalith is perfectly symmetrical. But very often the monument is in the shape of a 'p' or a 'q', according to whether the chamber lies to the right or to the left of the passage.

Figs. 6, 7, 8

The chamber itself varies in shape. It is usually circular; when the orthostats that frame it are set at clearly defined angles

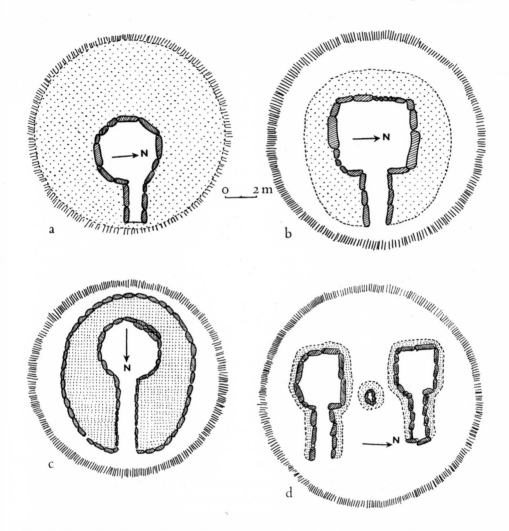

Fig. 6 Plans of the Passage Graves of: a, Parc-Guren, Crach (M.), with a circular chamber; b, Moulin-des-Oies Belz (M.), with a rectangular chamber; c, Mané-Bogat, Ploemel (M.), with a circular chamber and a long passage; and d, plan of the cairn of Roh-Vihan, La-Trinité-sur-Mer (M.), containing two Passage Graves with rectangular chambers, and a cist

to one another, it is rectangular or polygonal. In the latter case one of the sides is formed by a large block at right angles to the axis of the passage. There are also trapezoidal chambers; with these, one of the sides of the monument is more or less rectilinear, from the passage entrance to the far end of the chamber.

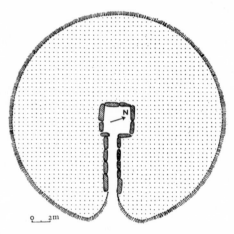

Fig. 7 Plan of the Passage Grave of Kercado, Carnac (M.), with a square chamber and a long passage

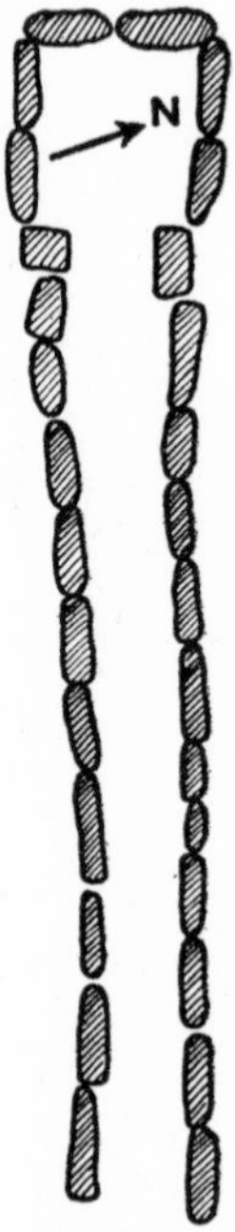

The other side runs parallel to the first in the passage part, then diverges sharply to form the chamber. Sometimes the two sides diverge from the entrance of the passage to the far end of the chamber. The transition from passage to chamber is then marked by a transverse stone sharply reducing the width of the passage. The size of the chamber varies considerably; the smallest passage graves have a chamber with an area of 3 to 4 sq. m., the largest are up to 16 sq. m. in area. The variations in plan are due chiefly to the materials used. Generally, Breton Passage Graves are built with large blocks of stone. The larger the orthostats, the more difficult it is to build a circular chamber, which consequently becomes rectangular or polygonal.

Fig. 8a Plan of the Passage Grave of Gavrinis, Larmor-Baden (M.), with a long passage. $\frac{1}{200}$

Not all the Passage Graves, however, were built of orthostats. Very often the passage and chamber were constructed with dry stone walling. With such material, the chambers were usually circular or oval. Walls of this kind were sometimes reinforced with orthostats used as buttresses inside.

In some cases, in particular the Passage Grave of Ile-Carn, Ploudalmezeau (Finistère),[8] where the passage and chamber are of dry stones, the passage was completely closed at both ends by a little wall of the same construction. In other instances there may simply be a rough filling-in.

To cover over the dry stone walled chambers, corbelling is often resorted to. This corbelled structure is shaped like a cone, sometimes quite high, its crest surmounted by a somewhat larger stone. In a few examples the corbelling only produces a fairly low truncated cone, with a very large slab on the top. The Passage Graves whose walls comprise large slabs are roofed over in two different ways. Usually a large flat stone has been rolled directly on to the orthostats. These covering stones are sometimes of enormous size; at Mané-Rutual and Mané-Lud, Locmariaquer (Morbihan), they are considerably larger than the area of the chamber. There are fairly frequent instances, however, of a corbelled structure having been built on the orthostats, perhaps for lack of sufficiently large covering stones.

Many of the Passage Graves that are now open to the sky must have been covered originally by a corbelled roof which has since been destroyed. If they had been covered by a capstone, the ceiling would often have been definitely too low; whatever system of roofing was used, the inner height of the chambers is always greater than that of the passages. It happens, moreover, that even the passages are lower at their entrance than at the point where they reach the chamber.

The Passage Graves are usually paved in some way. The paving can vary from flat stones, carefully arranged, as at Gavrinis, and at Mané-Lud, Locmariaquer to simple beds of stones, well levelled, as at Barnenez, Plouézoc'h. Before the

Plates 5, 6

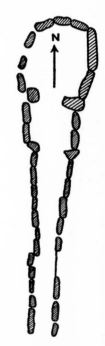

Fig. 8b Plan of the Passage Grave of Mané-Rutual, Locmariaquer (M.), with chamber and antechamber. $\frac{1}{200}$

stones were laid the ground was levelled either with ballast or packed clay.

The orientation of the Passage Graves has both a variable and a constant factor. For, whilst they do not all run in exactly the same direction, the axis nearly always lies between 90° and 180°—that is, the opening of the passage faces east, east-south-east, south-east, south-south-east or south. A very few open to the north, as does the small tomb of Conguel, Quiberon (Morbihan).

Passage Graves as we now know them may or may not have a covering mound. Where a mound exists, it covers the monu-ment entirely, particularly in the case of Passage Graves with an intact corbelled roof; but this also may be so with the trabeated roofed chambers. The mounds of many of the Passage Graves are only as high as the capstones. Here, it is difficult to know whether it is the remains of a covering mound which has been worn down, or whether it is only a construction mound needed in order to put the capstones in their places; even a total disappearance of the mound is not ruled out.

The Passage Graves have round mounds, except where there are several of them side by side under the same mound. These may be built of a pile of stones round the tomb, finished off with a covering of earth, or it may be a cairn entirely built of stone. The corbelled vaults, moreover, rely for their support on the mass of stones accumulated round them. The cairn may be revetted by a series of concentric walls; one, in particular, is to be found level with the entrance to the passage.

When the Passage Grave is long, its chamber is usually found in the centre of the mound, directly beneath the summit, and the passage emerges at the end of the mound. Passage Graves with shorter passages may either have the chamber in the centre, so that the passage does not emerge, or the chamber is thrown off-centre sufficiently for the entrance to the passage to come fairly near the edge of the mound.

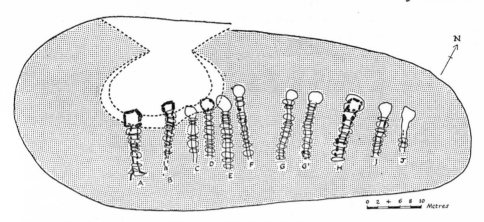

Fig. 9 Plan of the great cairn of Barnenez, Plouézoc'h (F.), containing eleven Passage Graves side by side

Although normally there is only one Passage Grave in a round mound, one occasionally encounters two or three together, so arranged as to take up the least room. They usually all face the same way (Rondossec, Plouharnel, Morbihan), and the passages emerge on the same side. At Mané-Kerioned, Carnac (Morbihan), however, the three Passage Graves are arranged in a horseshoe, two being parallel, and the third lying between the other two at right angles to them. On the Ile-Guennoc, Landeda (Finistère), there are numerous small Passage Graves side by side, but they are grouped in several small adjoining mounds, forming a row of a dozen monuments.

Plate 9

The larger cairn at Barnenez, Plouézoc'h[9], on the other hand, has eleven Passage Graves under a single mound, which is elongated because of the side-by-side disposition of the graves. This group is particularly interesting because it demonstrates a whole variety of constructional styles. Chambers roofed over by corbelling are found next to ones covered with a single slab. Some employ large blocks, others small stones. The corbelling

Fig. 9

D

Plates 5, 6

may be either steep or gradual in profile, and may rest on circular dry stone walls or on large orthostats. Sometimes the passages are built of dry stones, elsewhere they are strengthened by buttresses applied to a wall of masonry. One of these passages is specially interesting because its structure is rather unusual for Armorica: preceding the chamber is an ante-chamber, which, situated at the end of a passage built by the dry stone method with buttresses, is constructed with dry stones faced with false orthostats, whilst the chamber itself is built with enormous functional orthostats, supporting an impressive covering slab. All the passages of this vast cairn open towards the south-east.

The fine monuments of Barnenez show by the way they are juxtaposed that in spite of its fairly numerous variations the simple Passage Grave derives from a single basic type. The variations are no doubt due to the exigencies of construction or to the whim of the builders; in no case do they constitute a typological series.

THE ART OF THE PASSAGE GRAVES

There are fairly numerous examples of decorated Passage Graves in Armorica, particularly in Morbihan—about a score in all;[10] this decoration consists chiefly of designs engraved on the slabs of which the megalithic tombs are built—either on the orthostats or on the capstones. The engraving was carried out in widely varying ways. In some cases, the lines have been very

Plates 39, 40

deeply pecked and well weathered, especially at Gavrinis, Larmor-Baden; in others the rock has simply been marked with dots, and the design has no relief. The latter type of decoration relies only upon difference in tone, and may have an astonishing freshness. Passage Grave H, at Barnenez, shows both these techniques.

Sculptured decorations are relatively rare; but some of the

Fig. 10

stones of the Gavrinis monument have them (triangular axes with splayed cutting edge), as has also a stone of the Petit-Mont

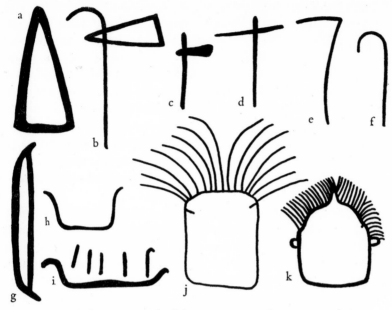

Fig. 10 Principal elementary motifs of the ornamentation of Passage Graves: a, axe without handle; b, c, d, hafted axes; e, f, crook; g, bow; h, yoke-sign; i, boat; j, k, buckler motif

Passage Grave, Arzon (two feet in relief, in a rectangular cartouche—believed by some authors to have been executed at a later period than the Passage Graves).

The art of the Passage Graves employs a number of different motifs, which are presented in a great many variations.

The axe is certainly one of the most frequent themes. It is usually in the form of a vertical or horizontal isosceles triangle, without any morphological details. However, the Gavrinis axes have a definitely splayed cutting edge, and can be related to the axes found in the big mounds of the Carnac district, much later than this period. The triangles are always vertical when no handle is represented; where there is a handle, they

Plate 40

Plate 11
Plate 12

can be either vertical or horizontal. The handle is indicated by a single line, the end nearest the axe-head being curved like a crook; examples of this can be seen at Mané-Kerioned, and at Petit-Mont, Arzon. At the Table-des-Marchands, Locmaria-quer (Morbihan), and at Gavrinis, Larmor-Baden, the handle is drawn with a double line, and one can make out a ring for attachment or hanging. Representations on the tombs of Penhap, Ile-aux-Moines, and of Mané-Rutual, Locmariaquer (Morbihan), are possibly also axes with handles. The marks in the form of a cross, somewhat unsymmetrical, which are found comparatively frequently, are also believed to be very stylised axes or adzes with their handles.

The U- or double U-shaped sign occurs with similar frequency; it is usually interpreted as a yoke, or as representing the horns of cattle. Whilst it is often found singly, it is not unusual for several yokes to be grouped together or super-imposed, as at Mané-Lud, Locmariaquer, where they are particularly numerous.

In some of the Morbihan Passage Graves one finds a design resembling a boat with a high prow and poop, and vertical lines representing the masts, though this interpretation is doubtful and not universally accepted. At Petit-Mont, Arzon, this ship, without a mast, has been given a 'sail'. Perhaps these alleged ships were ceremonial vessels carrying away the souls of the dead.

To protect the remains of the dead from evil spirits or grave-robbers, one of the orthostats in chamber H at Barnenez, has a bow engraved upon it, placed so that it appears to shoot towards the passage, the only normal approach to the tomb.

Plate 40

Wavy or broken lines are plentiful in some of the monu-ments; they are found set both vertically or horizontally. At Gavrinis, Larmor-Baden, they clearly represent serpents facing one another, with definitely individual heads. When the lines are horizontal, they may, perhaps, represent stylised waves.

One of the most interesting motifs is the ogival one known as the buckler motif (or figure in the form of a cooking-pot), which may be in the shape of a trapeze, a triangle, or the arc of a circle. This design is found in conjunction with various accessory elements, either separately or together: diverging lines, long or short, above it; a pointed beak; lateral 'handles' or 'ears', and notches immediately above the ears. This motif has often been interpreted as a stylisation of the Mother-Goddess, with hair, nose and ears. Sometimes it has been regarded as a cooking-pot with handles, and with ears of wheat protruding from it. Again, it has been suggested that it might be the sail of a ship (it is in association with a supposed ship's hull at Petit-Mont, Arzon); in that case the beak would represent the top of the mast, the 'hairs' would be streamers floating in the wind, the notches and handles would be for attaching the rigging. The size and position of this complicated figure varies. At Mané-Rutual, Locmariaquer, it is engraved beneath the large capstone of the chamber, and is enormous. At Table-des-Marchands, the whole large orthostat at the end of the chamber, ogival in shape, represents the 'sail'; on its rear surface are engraved a central ring and lateral rings, while on its front surface is a shield decorated with streamers on the outside, and on the inside with four rows of crooks in relief, distributed on either side of the vertical axis, where there are other more indistinct signs.

Plate 13

Some of the symbols are extremely difficult to interpret. Among these are the lines which cross one another without any apparent order; the general appearance is of a survey or topographical map, and this is the most favoured hypothesis. The crook-shaped lines and the angles, simple though they appear, are just as difficult to understand. Perhaps they are simply derived from axe or adze signs.

The purely geometrical designs, such as the concentric half-circles, do not present such a problem. The Gavrinis Passage

Grave is plentifully decorated with them; each support has a veritable decorative panel executed with extraordinary skill. Instead of exhibiting engravings juxtaposed without any apparent order, as is often the case in the large Passage Graves (Mané-Lud, Locmariaquer, for example), the motifs are arranged in a very elaborate composition.

Apart from Gavrinis, the decoration of Passage Graves does not appear to be particularly elaborate; it is not without interest, however, because it may represent certain abstract ideas, revealing themselves in a naïve stylisation of commonplace objects—a stylisation which we are not always in a position to understand and which could readily be misinterpreted.

THE DATING OF THE PASSAGE GRAVES As they were used and re-used over a long period and were subsequently plundered on several occasions, Passage Graves do not usually offer much material which could help in establishing the date of their erection.

An exception is the corbelled Passage Grave of Ile-Carn, Ploudalmezeau (Finistère), doubly sealed in and containing only three dozen true Neolithic sherds and a few flints, together with some charcoal fragments; it was probably used once or twice before being covered up in the centre of its huge cairn. The charcoal found in the chamber, on and between the paving stones, has been dated to 3030±75 B.C. by means of the radiocarbon method. This date fits in very well with the date 3140± 60 B.C. already quoted for the dwelling site of Curnic, Guissény, whose inhabitants were certainly megalith builders.[11]

Thus the Passage Graves in Brittany began well before 3000 B.C. (and therefore must have begun even earlier in Iberia, although no radio-carbon date is yet available), very shortly after the start of the Atlantic Western Neolithic Culture. This is a very important and exciting conclusion even if it does not fit in with the 'short' chronological systems that were until recently in fashion.

CHAPTER IV

The Armorican Chalcolithic Culture

PREHISTORIANS HAVE by no means underestimated the importance of the appearance of the earliest objects made in metal; but the chronological position of these objects has been interpreted in various ways. Some writers have attributed them to the early part of the Bronze Age; others have created a Copper Age immediately preceding the Bronze Age. We have preferred to adopt a contemporary view which places a Chalcolithic culture straddling the two main phases of the Neolithic cultures.[1] We are therefore concerned here with a first diffusion of metal, on a fairly limited scale, quite distinct from the period of the Early and Middle Bronze Age barrow culture where metal is comparatively plentiful.

The Chalcolithic culture manifests itself with the appearance of objects made of arsenical copper, western European tanged daggers and flat axes, objects of gold, and some other types of implements, all associated with Bell Beaker pottery. In Armorica, this diffusion seems to be distinct from that of the early megaliths, and later in date; but this in no way prevents the Bell Beaker complex from being found in graves together with material which is purely Neolithic or late Neolithic.

There seems to be no doubt about the Spanish ancestry of the Armorican Bell Beakers (*vases campaniformes*). The Galician group of beakers, though not very large, unquestionably offers the closest analogy to the Armorican group; in fact, there is a very striking resemblance between them. The link must have been a maritime one, as was quite usual at this period.

The Armorican series can be divided arbitrarily into two groups: a series of 'prototypes', and a series of imitations, although this division has no chronological implications.

BELL
BEAKER
POTTERY

Fig. 11

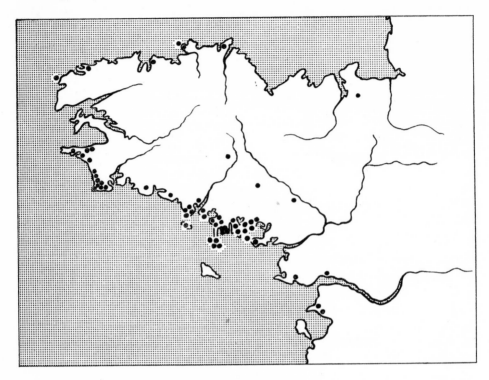

Fig. 11 Distribution map of Bell Beakers

Plates 14, 15 The 'prototype' pots are very beautiful, both on account of their decoration and the fineness of the ware. They are red or orange in colour, embellished by a burnished slip; the lines of the decoration, carried out while the clay is soft, are sometimes encrusted with a white substance which makes the pattern show up clearly. The paste is very homogeneous, red, and extremely well fired. The forms are constant; the base is slightly concave, the profile S-shaped with varying degrees of curvature so that sometimes the walls of the pots are almost vertical and sometimes extremely undulating. The pots are therefore very

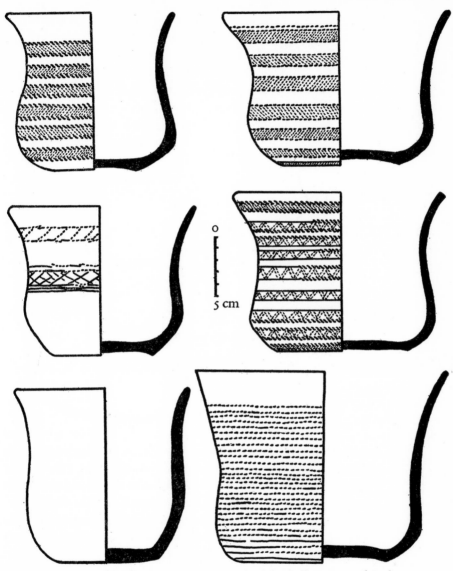

Fig. 12 Forms and decoration of the Bell Beakers from the Gallery Grave of Kerbors (C. du N.)

Fig. 12 varied; some are tall and slender, others full-bodied. The rims are all simple.

The decoration of this Beaker pottery is classical; the same designs are found in the south of France and in Iberia. These consist essentially of pointillé ornament made with the roulette or with a square-toothed comb. On some pots one can establish the length of the comb and the number of teeth. Rather

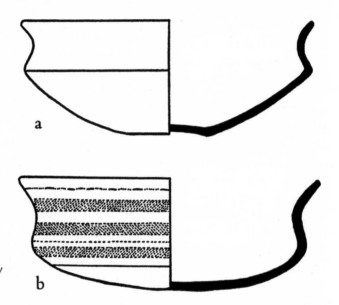

a

b

Fig. 13 a, Carinated bowl and b, bowl with Beaker decoration, from the Gallery Grave of Kerbors. Both $\frac{1}{6}$

less frequently, little cords have been used, leaving characteristic rows of oblique impressions. Although the patterns are fairly varied, they can be divided into a few definite types. They consist of parallel lines which are sometimes complete in themselves; more often, they serve to outline alternating bands of hatching, in oblique dotted lines which run in alternate directions. The hatching may be replaced by a light criss-crossing, by triangles, or by dents-de-loup. More rarely, chequered patterns occur with several rows of opposed triangles.

These handsome beakers were widely imitated by local potters, who, however, copied them in a very clumsy fashion— no doubt because they were used to fashioning rough vessels such as the Late Neolithic 'flower-pots'. The ware is often thick and badly fired, burnished or unburnished, lustreless, yellow or brownish; the *dégraissant* is often similar to that of Late Neolithic pots: it contains large fragments of quartz and mica. Its general appearance is crude, but the forms remain typical. The decoration is similar, also carried out with a comb or a cord, but it is not so clear; the pattern is hesitant and badly imprinted because of the irregularity of the ware.

The Gallery Grave of Men-ar-Rompet, Kerbors (Côtes-du-Nord),[2] has yielded a large bowl, almost intact, which certainly belongs to the Beaker group of pottery. It has an S profile, flattened down on account of its considerable size. It is of exactly the same ware as the fine Beaker pots, and its decoration is typical—parallel lines with oblique dotted hatching. This bowl is not so very different from the 'cazuelas' of the Iberian peninsula, particularly those from the cemetery of Ciempozuelos. It should be pointed out that the same monument (Kerbors) and the tomb of Grah-Niol, Arzon (Morbihan), have produced fragments of other decorated dishes of the same type.

The monuments of Crugou, Plovan (Finistère), and of Kerbors, have yielded other large vessels, differing in shape from those described above. They also differ from the numerous carinated dishes found at Renongar, Plovan (Finistère), and Kerugou, Plomeur (Finistère), which are characteristic of the Late Neolithic culture of Armorica. These bowls have a clearly marked carination, and a flat or slightly concave base. They have no decoration, either dotted or channelled. The ware is reddish or brownish, usually fairly thin, and almost identical with the beautiful beakers. In Armorica, these dishes therefore belong to the Chalcolithic culture, but seem to be relatively rare local adaptations of vases of the Renongar or Kerugou types.

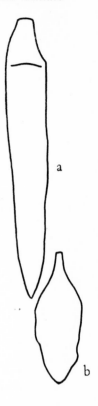

Fig. 14 West European daggers of arsenicated copper: a, long type, from the Gallery Grave of Penker, Plozévet (F.); b, short type (Palmella point) from the Passage Grave of Kercadoret, Locmariaquer (M.). Both ½

There are several objects which usually accompany the Bell Beakers: small, flat-tanged western European daggers, archers' wrist-guards, and buttons with V-shaped perforations. Actually it is very rare to find all these objects together; in this respect the grave-goods of the Gallery Grave of Penker, Plozévet (Finistère), are exceptional since, in addition to items from the Late Neolithic cultures, the grave contained a beaker, a dagger of arsenical copper, a wrist-guard, and a button with V-perforation. In the Gallery Grave of Kerandrèze, Moëlan (Finistère), two elements were associated—a dagger and a wrist-guard. Everywhere else, only a single object has been found in association with beakers.

Fig. 14
The flat-tanged *West European daggers* are the only metal objects directly linked with beakers. There are not many of these in Brittany; we have been able to list only eleven, both in bibliographies and collections, and some are of doubtful authenticity.[3] Typologically, there are two main kinds: a short one (7 to 8 cm.) with clearly differentiated flat tang, and a long one (12 to 15 cm.) where the tang is not usually very distinct. The dagger from Penker, Plozévet, one of the long variety, bears traces of a hafting, now lost, but clearly indicating the tang. The short daggers with well-defined tang seem to mark the transition to the javelin-heads, of which an example was found at Trentemoult in the Loire near Nantes, in association

Plate 25
with flat axes. This object is fairly close to the dagger from the megalithic tomb of Kercadoret, Locmariaquer (Morbihan), and belongs to the same type as the Palmella points of Portugal. We possess only one full analysis of these daggers, based on the example found in Passage Grave C of Barnenez; this analysis reveals a high proportion of arsenic (2.34 per cent) and the metallographic examination shows that it was worked by hammering the heated metal.

Fig. 15
The archers' *wrist-guards* are plaques of schist, usually rectangular; one face is convex, the other flat. These objects were

used to protect the wrist of an archer from the recoil of the bowstring and of course imply the use of this type of weapon. They are pierced at each end with a biconical hole, to enable them to be held in place. Here again there are two types: short and wide (60⁄80 by 30⁄35 mm.), or long and narrow (110 by

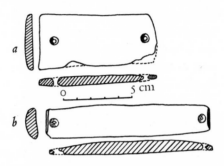

Fig. 15 Wrist-guards of polished schist with two holes: a, short type, from the Passage Grave of Kerallant, Saint-Jean-Brévelay (M.); b, long type, from the Gallery Grave of Kerbors (C.-du-N.)

25 mm.). Thirteen wrist-guards have been found in Brittany; no doubt one should classify with these a gold plaque found at Mané-Lud, Locmariaquer (Morbihan). It has six small holes at each end, and was probably originally attached to some piece of organic material.

The *buttons with V-perforation*, being made of bone, are very rare in Armorica, because conditions do not favour the preservation of this material. Of the four we know, only the one from the Gallery Grave of Penker, Plozévet is a true V-button, and unfortunately it is broken. Those found at Er-Lannic, Arzon (Morbihan) and in the Passage Grave of Kerioret, Saint-Jean-Trolimon (Finistère) have quite a special character; there is a small shank beneath the cap, perforated transversally—a purely local adaptation.

As practically everywhere in western Europe, Bell Beakers occur in Brittany in association with elements of other cultures. In the Passage Graves, they generally accompany Neolithic CONTEXT AND DIS- TRIBUTION pottery, rather late in type; in the Gallery Graves they occur together with carinated vessels and Late Neolithic 'flower-pots'. Thus, at Barnenez, where the eleven juxtaposed Passage Graves were built near the conclusion of the genuine Neolithic culture, the beakers in tombs C and D may well be contemporary with some pottery of Western type. On the other hand, the fine material from the Gallery Grave of Penker, Plozévet, was found associated with polished axes, pendants, and pottery of the Late Neolithic culture.

The Beaker culture, therefore, was simply superimposed on Western megalithic civilisations, and was adopted by them. That is why the earliest models of pots, very handsome and perfectly resembling the Spanish prototypes, were followed by a series of imitations where local techniques were immediately apparent. As the earliest beakers were no doubt introduced at the time of transition from the Neolithic culture to the Late Neolithic culture, it is not surprising to find them in a very wide context, both in the simple and more highly evolved Passage Graves and in the Gallery Graves. Their geographical distribution is therefore coupled with that of the megaliths. The empty zones in the interior of the country simply correspond to our total lack of knowledge about the contents of the graves there.

AWLS AND VARIOUS METAL OBJECTS

Three awls have been found in Passage Graves: one at Port-Blanc, Saint-Pierre-Quiberon (Morbihan), another at Beg-er-Lann, Ploemeur (Morbihan), and the third and last in the barrow of La Motte, Pornic (Loire-Atlantique). These are little pointed instruments, with quadrangular or lozenge-shaped stems, no doubt made of arsenical copper. At Port-Blanc and at La Motte they were found in association with Beaker pottery; in all three cases Late Neolithic pottery was also found; genuine Neolithic was found only at Port-Blanc. In southern France, where they are plentiful in megalithic tombs, the awls are clearly Chalcolithic; in spite of their scarcity, this is also probably the case in Armorica.

In the angled Passage Grave of Luffang, Crach (Morbihan), a copper spiral has been found which may also belong to the Chalcolithic culture.

A certain number of gold objects are attributed to the Chalcolithic culture;[4] these have mostly been found in megalithic tombs, especially in the Passage Graves of a simple type or with side chambers. Two bracelets have been found at the foot of a menhir, at SaintCado, Belz (Morbihan).

The most beautiful ornaments are undoubtedly the wellknown bracelets from the Rondossec Passage Graves, Plouharnel (Morbihan). They were found in a pot, and are peculiar in that their central part is cut into fine ribbons. One of them is also decorated on the sides. The two ends are bent back to form a fastening. A slightly larger bracelet came from a Passage Grave at SaintPèreenRetz (LoireAtlantique) and was associated with two flat copper axes. In the same monument was found a little gold ring, fastening with a hook and eyelet, and also two fragments of a ribbon torque with terminals. The bracelets from SaintCado, Belz, completely solid and undecorated, have a slightly more advanced system of hooks: the two bentback ends are tapered and perpendicular.

A curved gold object found in a Gallery Grave on the Gras Heath, Meslin (CôtesduNord), may have been a sort of diadem. A band 21 by 1·4 cm. from the Passage Grave of Kerouaren, Plouhinec (Morbihan), has a row of holes all round it, and must have been attached to a piece of cloth or leather, to form a headband or a dress ornament.

Various other gold objects, less spectacular but just as interesting, have also been found. A globular bead, formed of two hollow hemispheres joined together, decorated with concentric lines, comes from a Passage Grave at Kermarquer,

La-Trinité-sur-Mer (Morbihan). Small flat circular pieces with two or four holes in the centre may have been button facings; they very closely resemble some Portuguese gold discs. The tubular beads are small thin sheets of hammered gold bent round so that they can be threaded on to a string; some are decorated. About a dozen examples are known; eight of them came from the La-Motte mound, Pornic. Four scalloped plaques have been found in the Passage Grave of Kerlagat, Carnac (Morbihan). Two have four teeth, the other two have five; all have a hole at each end for attaching them to something.

The spirals are thin threads of gold twisted into coils of vary-ing degrees of slackness. They are probably related to the copper spirals, one example of which has already been mentioned. A dozen little gold plaques with turned-in edges have been found in various Passage Graves in Morbihan; finally, one may men-tion a variety of small gold objects including wires and a nugget.

Objects made of precious metal have been found almost exclusively along the Atlantic seaboard, which was the area of maximum concentration of beakers and the objects associated with them. Whilst we cannot conclude from this that there is a definite connexion between gold and the Beaker complex, it is fairly certain that their diffusion was contemporaneous.

FLAT AXES The flat copper axes have rarely been found in hoards; where this was the case, the number found together was not very great. It is true that seventy axes were recorded at Plou-daniel (Finistère), but this should be accepted with caution. Eight or nine in a hoard seems to be the maximum.

Flat axes are sometimes found near megalithic monuments and dwelling sites (the camp of Lizo, Carnac, Morbihan). More often, they are surface finds.

Typologically, there is a certain variety of shapes and sizes. Those with an irregular and blistered surface have sometimes been regarded as rough castings. Such a phenomenon may be the result of electrolytic changes of the metal in the ground, and a thorough metallographic examination may in some cases show a structure resulting from the metal being worked cold and then reheated. However, some axes have no functional cutting edge; the end does not taper, and the thickness here makes it unfit for working with. These would be rough-outs, not rough castings, analogous to the bipennate ingots of Central Europe.

There are functional axes of a primitive type, whose cutting edge is effective, the butt being rounded and the sides straight or even convex. The advanced types have a rectangular butt; here the cutting edge may be splayed, while the sides are concave. A few thin examples, with hammered edges, have a very slight rim, and are fairly close to some early Bronze Age types.

Plate 25

It is, in fact, very exceptional to find flat axes among the grave-goods in the megalithic tombs of Brittany. We have no precise data on the flat axe discovered in the cemetery of Lesconil, Plobannalec (Finistère). At Saint-Père-en-Retz, moreover, where two axes were found with some gold objects beneath a tomb, it is possible that these items were in fact a later hoard, and not primary funerary material.

Carvings of axes with splayed blades are sometimes put forward as proof that the flat axes and some of the megalithic monuments were contemporaneous. The Passage Grave of Gavrinis, Larmor-Baden (Morbihan), is a good example of this. In addition, one must not forget that the flat axes gave rise to very fine imitations in polished stone, of which many examples are found among the grave-goods of the large mounds in the Carnac region.

Objects are rarely found in association with the flat axes; obviously one must disregard the examples where these have been recovered and included in hoards of a later period. The hoard at Trentemoult, near Nantes (Loire-Atlantique), is extremely interesting; a javelin head or Palmella point was found in association with nine flat axes. This Palmella point is

Plate 25

E

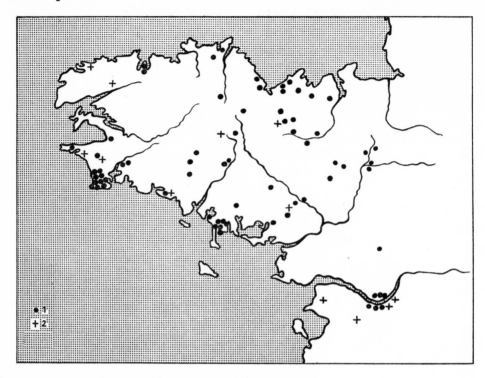

Fig. 16 Distribution map of flat axes: 1, isolated finds; 2, hoards

very close to the daggers of the Beaker complex, and occurs relatively often in the Chalcolithic cultures of western Iberia. The Plouguerneau (Finistère) hoard is much more doubtful; it contained two flat axes, two copper wires bent into hooks, and six daggers of the type known as Cypriot. It is the presence of these daggers that is awkward, although the Gallery Grave of Le-Tertre-de-l'Eglise, Plévenon (Côtes-du-Nord), produced a weapon of fairly similar type, and, as we shall see, carved representations of daggers which resemble them quite closely decorate several of the Gallery Graves of Brittany.

From the metallurgical point of view, it should be noted that the flat axes are usually of arsenical copper,[5] the arsenic content sometimes being as high as 4 per cent, and there is a definite relationship with Chalcolithic objects also made of copper alloyed with arsenic. Thus there is a flat axe, discovered in Finistère, whose composition is nearly identical to that of the western European dagger of Barnenez, even where the various impurities are concerned. The presence of some arsenic gives to copper a certain hardness, and this combination can be wrought when heated, unlike bronze. It is difficult to believe that it is a true determined alloy; more probably it is the result of the empirical choice of favourable ores, with a high arsenic content.

The geographical distribution of the flat axes is bounded to the east by the Vilaine; their maximum concentration coincides with that of the megaliths. The Loire estuary also contains an important concentration, which links Brittany to Vendée and Anjou—other regions prolific in flat axes. The distribution of flat axes and of beakers each show the same concentrations on the south side of Armorica. This latter area must have received the prototypes, wherever they came from, and they were then carried into the interior regions. The flat axes also spread as far as Penthièvre, in a district where the Gallery Graves are fairly plentiful.

Fig. 16

CHAPTER V

The Late Neolithic Cultures of Armorica

THE FULLY DEVELOPED Late Neolithic culture is essentially characterised by a pottery of coarse ware and fairly simple forms, and by a new type of megalithic tomb—the Gallery Grave. However, there is no definite break between the Neolithic and the Late Neolithic cultures. On the contrary, the ceramic forms of the Neolithic continue to be produced, in a more clumsy ware, alongside the new forms, and the Passage Graves are still widely used and more complex types are evolved. As a result, the transition between Neolithic and Late Neolithic cultures is rather vague and indefinite. With the information at present at our disposal it is impossible to be more precise. There may be Middle Neolithic cultural elements, but more radio-carbon dates are necessary before this can be stated with certainty.

The Late Neolithic is not, therefore, simply a belated leap forward; nor is it a late cultural spread, such as occurred else-where in Europe, of peoples who had remained at the Meso-lithic stage; it is, in fact, the most important and longest phase of the Armorican Neolithic.[1] Its duration is further accentuated by the fact that its upper limit does not coincide with the lower limit of the Early Bronze Age. Indeed, the native inhabitants carried on their traditions long after the introduction of the Bronze Age barrow culture, and parallel to the latter. The evidence suggests that these traditions died out during the early part of the Middle Bronze Age.

LATE NEOLITHIC POTTERY Unlike Neolithic pottery, which was usually thin, slipped, well fired and fairly elaborate in form, the pottery of the Late Neolithic culture—an Armorican facies of the Seine-Oise-Marne type of pottery—is coarse and not very well finished.[2]

The ware is very thick, and badly fired, as shown in section, by the presence of a black layer between two red layers. It is not burnished, and the *dégraissant* is very crude; quartz and felspar gravel can be seen on the broken edges, making the surface of the vessels very rough.

As regards the forms, one must not confuse those which are typical of this culture, and which are also found in the Seine-Oise-Marne culture (and its extensions towards the Loire, the Vienne and the Charente), with those which are imitations of archaic forms.

The typical shapes are simple—pots commonly known as 'flower-pots'. The base is flat, widening slightly; the body wide, sometimes misshapen and asymmetrical. The rims are simple, straight or curved slightly outwards. Long handles or thick cordons may sometimes break the general line of the body. The pots vary in size from small goblets or bowls 5 cm. high, with wide openings, to enormous jars 30 cm. or more high. As these pots are made by the coiled technique, and the handles and cordons simply applied to the body of the jar, these sometimes became detached when the clay dried, or the coils separated.

Plate 17

The other forms, less rough, were mostly taken over from those which already existed in Brittany and other regions during the period of the Neolithic culture. The round-bottomed pots were widely produced again, in the form of medium-sized bowls with round bases and straight edges. These never have a neck. Where there are handles, these are just clumsy knobs. Fairly large numbers have been found in the Gallery Graves of the Côtes-du-Nord, where there are not many traces of pure Neolithic culture; also in the southern Finistère tombs and in Morbihan, where collective graves were in use for a very long time.

The pure Neolithic facies in Brittany produced none of the carinated forms such as occur in the Chassey or Windmill Hill cultures. These make a late appearance, in a fairly homogeneous ware, coarser than that of the Breton Neolithic, but not nearly

Plates 18, 22

so thick as the rough Late Neolithic forms. The bases are round or flat, and the carination well marked. Two definite series exist: pots of modest size, with straight, simple edges, and large dishes with a low profile and slightly curved rims. Their distribution coincides with that of the late round-bottomed vessels; that is to say, they are found as often in the Gallery Graves of the Côtes-du-Nord as in the Passage Graves and Gallery Graves of southern Finistère and Morbihan.

The 'flower-pots' have no decoration to speak of. Sometimes there are just a few marks made with finger-nails, without any particular arrangement. Fairly evenly spaced imprints of fingers on the rim and on the relief cordons also occur.

The other vessels—round-bottomed bowls or carinated dishes—which form a large collection in Armorica, are, however, all the more interesting because they are decorated, whether carinated or not; but it must be pointed out that the decorated pots derive from graves on the south side of Armorica, in the zone where the Passage Graves of simple or evolved types, and Western Neolithic pottery, are concentrated. This signifies that in this region the traditions of the Neolithic were strongly maintained. In the Côtes-du-Nord, on the other hand, the clumsy round-bottomed and carinated pots have no decoration; they have inherited the old Neolithic tradition only in their forms.

The decoration consists mainly of ribs and roughly executed channelling. The ribs are found in groups of 3, 4, 5 or 6, on the carinated pots only, and are arranged vertically between the carination and the rim. The channelling is quite unlike that on the true 'channelled ware' and more in the nature of incisions.

Plate 19

The lines are deeply scored into the ware, but their edges are irregular, evidently because of the coarseness and granular nature of the clay. On the carinated pots these incisions are either vertical, in groups, or horizontal. The small tomb of Conguel,

Plates 20, 21

Quiberon (Morbihan), has produced a very interesting and

typical series of round-bottomed pots decorated with incisions. The patterns vary; parallel lines, *dents de loup*, concentric semi-circles or arcs. These patterns and the pottery which they adorn are remarkably homogeneous; however these incised patterns may be arranged, a relationship is always clearly evident.

The impressive series of fragments of vase-supports found on the little islet of Er-Lannic, Arzon, in the gulf of Morbihan, probably belongs to the same period.[3] These vase-supports are round; their height varies between 3 and 11 cm., and their upper diameter between 13 and 20 cm. The upper surface is concave, the edge flat. Some vase-supports have triangular, rectangular or circular perforations on their circumference. Most have *pointillé* decoration, forming patterns of triangles, chequer-board designs, festoons or wavy lines. Of primary importance is the large amount of such pottery on this site; although in a fragmentary state, at least 160 different specimens have been listed from the excavation of part of the site. Only about ten other vase-supports are known in Morbihan, and none elsewhere in Armorica. It is difficult to establish whether these are ritual objects, or whether they were actually used at this site to support vases. In the latter case, they were designed to support round-bottomed pots, of which very few remains have been found at Er-Lannic, though there are plenty of fragments of coarse ware of the classical Late Neolithic style. In spite of the contexts in which the vase-supports of southern and eastern France are found, it would be rash to place those of Er-Lannic in the primordial Neolithic culture; they are coeval, rather, with the decorated round-bottomed pots of the Conguel type, and with the carinated bowls. In fact, all this pottery, though in the initial Neolithic tradition, is clearly influenced by Late Neolithic techniques.

Still more permeated by Late Neolithic techniques are certain pots whose origin has been sought by some authors in the Early Neolithic Age of the north of Europe (especially

Fig. 17

Denmark).[4] These are the 'collared flasks'. Their Breton context is clearly Late Neolithic; they have been found in re-used
Passage Graves and also in the Gallery Graves. They differ
from the Danish 'prototypes' in having acquired a flat base,
and in being made in the heavy 'flower-pot' ware. Moreover,
the collar is not so tight, and the profile less regular. The pot

Plate 24   from the Gallery Grave of Mélus, Ploubazlanec (Côtes-du-
Nord), is the most typical of the series; below the collarette are
nine large bosses, which seems to provide good grounds for
connecting it with a '*Kragenflasche*' found at Mellenballe in
Denmark. Another '*Kragenflasche*' discovered at Gellenerdeich,
near Oldenburg, has a still closer resemblance to the Armorican specimen. The ware is coarse and the base flat, which is
remarkable; moreover, the shape of body is more or less the
same as that of the Mélus pot; the collarette is like those on the
vases from the Gallery Grave of Kergüntuil, Trégastel (Côtes-
du-Nord) and from the Passage Grave of Lann-Blaën,

Plate 23   Guidel (Morbihan). The latter have more degenerate profiles,
though they are still fairly close to those of the Nordic flasks.
As for the other two cases, the one from Trorioun, Lannilis
(Finistère), has no collarette, and the one from the Gallery
Grave of Kerandrèze, Moëlan (Finistère), is hardly more than
a goblet with a thick marginal rib.

Before considering the stone material, the frequent occurrence
in Late Neolithic tombs of clay spindle whorls should be
noted. These vary in size, the average diameter being about 5
cm. The most usual shape is biconical, with an axial hole; but
there are also examples with one side flat or slightly concave.

STONE AND   Transverse arrow-heads must have continued in use at least
BONE   during the transition between the Neolithic and Late Neolithic
MATERIAL   cultures. The sharp-edged arrows of the inhabitants of Morbihan are probably of this epoch. Typologically, they do not differ
from those of the Neolithic cultures which we have already

Fig. 17 Pots related to the so-called 'collared flasks': a and b, from the Gallery Grave of Kergüntuil, Trégastel (C.-du-N.); c, from the Passage Grave of Lann-Blaën, Guidel (M.); d, from the Gallery Grave of Mélus, Loguivy-de-la-Mer, Ploubazlanec (C.-du-N.); e, from the Gallery Grave of Kerandrèze, Moëlan (F.); f, from the megalithic tomb of Trorioun, Lannilis (F.)

described. At the time of maximum development of the Late Neolithic cultures, they disappear; none have been found in the Armorican Gallery Graves.

On the other hand, fairly highly developed barbed and tanged arrow-heads are found in Late Neolithic monuments. They are symmetrical, slender, with well defined barb and tang, but these are never as deeply notched as in the Early

Bronze Age barrows. The triangular form with a wide base is the most usual; the ogival form is rare; a few instances are known where the sides of the triangle are slightly concave (as from the Passage Grave with side chamber of Kermarker, La Trinité-sur-Mer, Morbihan). These arrows are always fairly thick.

The large blades, the knives and daggers in pale 'wax-coloured' flint, are definitely linked with the Late Neolithic complex. The knives are blades retouched on both sides; the daggers, thicker but not so wide, have one end tapered and very much retouched, ending in a more or less sharp point; their average length is about 17 cm. These objects are made of a special kind of flint, probably imported from Touraine (and hence called Grand-Pressigny flint). There are also some fine items in grey flint, from another distant source.

Plates 28, 29

All the other flint objects look much the same as similar items from the Neolithic culture. Only flakes with varying degrees of retouching are found in most of the graves. Habitat sites in Morbihan have produced scrapers of various kinds, and awls. The presence of one rather special object, the fabricator, should be noted in Late Neolithic contexts; it is a short, heavy tool 4 to 5 cm. long, with the thinner end blunted.

There is plenty of material made of stone other than flint—especially in the shape of 'polished axes' and pebble tools. In addition, there are pendants of various shapes; those most frequently found are rectangular, with a biconical hole at one end, but the discoid form is not rare. The most curious are those resembling little axes. These are never very thick. Various stones are used—fibrolite, quartz, greenstone, sometimes flint, as well as red schist. Some pendants follow a special style; they are shaped like a segment of a circle. Typically, these arc-pendants are pierced at each end; but they are usually broken and only one half has been found.

The earliest beads made of callaïs (a bluish phosphatic mineral of uncertain origin) appear in Passage Graves in the Carnac region which were re-utilised by the Late Neolithic people. They are no doubt related to the beads from the large Carnac mounds, but the shapes differ—as well as discoid beads there are also tubular ones, which are totally absent from the big Carnac mounds. Globular pendants of callaïs also occur.

As in the Neolithic culture, numerous makeshift tools in the shape of pebbles used as strikers and burnishers, as well as many grindstones and pestles for crushing grain, continue to be found.

Connected with the use of arrows, there were tools for straightening their shafts. These are stones (often the half of a split pebble) with a groove on the flat surface. This groove acted as a plane or a scraper-plane. We know of two examples of this type of tool in Armorica: one from the corbelled Passage Grave of Tossen-ar-Run, Yvias (Côtes-du-Nord), and the other from the cemetery of Lesconil, Plobannalec (Finistère). Both are in a late context; this type of tool, how-ever, is found elsewhere in Europe in all cultures where arrows were used.

The only important bone objects we know come from the islet of Er Yoh, near the island of Houat (Morbihan). They are chiefly polished axe-sleeves of classical type, made of antler or of the horns of cattle, and a certain number of flat bone imple-ments with rounded ends—one with a long bone handle, to make a retouching tool.[5] A few whistles have been found, made of the half of a sheep's jawbone, pierced and rounded.

Due to the unfavourable physico-chemical conditions, hardly any other bone objects have been found. But at Penhoët, Saint-Nazaire and Nantes (Loire-Atlantique) axes were dis-covered, fitted into an antler sleeve hafted with a wooden handle; another was dredged recently from the Lannion river (Côtes-du-Nord). In the river Odet an antler haft for a minute axe has been dredged up. And in a sub-littoral peaty deposit, now submerged, at Pléneuf (Côtes-du-Nord), there was a very fine pick,[6] also made from an antler, exactly on the classical model of tools used to dig the walls and galleries for extracting flint in chalk regions. Such objects must have been in common use.

This is an opportune moment for pointing out once for all that in studying these cultures, one should never lose sight of the fundamental rôle played by wooden equipment—though hardly anything remains of it except the tools with which the wood was cut, shaped or split.

THE 'POLISHED STONE AXES'

In flint-producing regions, sites, surface stations or Neolithic monuments produce unbelievable quantities of tools or prepa-ratory rough-outs in this material, which in weight or volume form the most elementarily classical aspect of Neolithic culture. In an ancient *massif* like Armorica, flint tools are rare, if not exceptional. The Neolithic objects, or those in the Neolithic tradition, which occur most frequently (and then not very abundantly) are those traditionally grouped under the name of 'polished stone axes', mostly made of hard stone of regional origin. Not only are they found fairly plentifully in Late Neolithic funerary monuments and sites (often in a fragmentary condition), but they are also the type of object most frequently picked up in the fields—perhaps simply because the farm workers recognise them, taking them for 'thunder-stones'. Examples are known from all parts of the province, and the number recorded or preserved depends largely on the activities of individual collectors who have taken the trouble to amass and classify them. Even so, one is struck by the extraordinary frequency with which 'polished stone axes' are discovered in certain regions, especially in the Bigouden area (Finistère), where nearly every field has produced some. From this one can deduce a considerable density of Late Neolithic population which had cleared and put under cultivation almost the whole region. Most of these implements must have been employed not

so much for 'chopping' wood or other materials as for agricultural purposes—to dig and plough the land, as well as to clear it.

From the morphological point of view, if we except the Plate 26
perforated implements discussed below, the Armorican 'axes'
vary fairly widely in shape, each form having its own slight
variations according to the type of stone and the method of
manufacture. The typical Armorican 'axe' has a pointed butt,
and a fairly thick oval section, tapering towards the cutting
edge. This type of object often has a long butt, and could be
fitted directly on to a wooden handle with a reinforced club-like
end. The blade may be vertical, and the 'axe' a true axe, but
there are also examples where the blade, which is curved on
both sides, is necessarily horizontal—the implement in this case
being either an adze or a kind of hoe. In addition to the perfect
forms of these long-heeled implements, a great many crudely-
fashioned, irregular and asymmetrical examples are found (not
very popular for displaying in museum show-cases); it seems
unlikely that they were used as tools for swinging (which
require to be reasonably well balanced). As well as hoes, one
wonders if some of the large examples could have been used as
ploughshares in a primitive kind of plough.

A great many axes, however, have a small rounded butt or
no butt at all. There is no doubt that these were fitted with a
handle by means of an intermediary sleeve of antler, itself perforated to take a wooden handle. It is noticeable that for the
same width of cutting edge, and therefore identical cutting
capacity, there are implements of widely varying lengths and
therefore of different weights. Some of these short tools even
have no cutting edge (or have one no longer), but a facet at
right angles to the axis, often finely polished. Used in the hand,
they may have served as polishers or burnishers, or, with a
handle, as hammers. A considerable number of very small tools
could have been used for fine work on wood, some of them as
chisels—unless they were toys or symbols, as suggested by the

frequency of tiny axes perforated at the butt so that they could be used as pendants.

It is rare to find rough-outs in flaked rocks like flint without traces of polishing. Some very tough rocks such as fibrolite could only be trimmed by sawing them out of lumps of natural mineral. Dyke rocks of the dolerite group are worked in the first instance by pecking and rough-hewing till a block of approximately the right shape is obtained. The tools were finished by polishing, but this was not always complete; sometimes it was only carried out at the cutting edge. Various highly finished axes, especially of flint or fibrolite, were polished in facets. Large fixed polishers of quartzite or sandstone are rare in Brittany; small portable ones were used more often, and some sites (especially Er-Lannic, Arzon, Morbihan) have provided numerous specimens of these.

BATTLE-
AXES
Fig. 18

The perforated implements, always fashioned of basic plutonic or metamorphic rocks, form a separate category. Heavy hammers, or hammer-axes, found very frequently in the north of Upper Brittany, no doubt reflect lake-dwelling influences on late Western Neolithic culture, and perhaps served a very practical purpose.

A difficult typological and genealogical problem is set by the battle-axes. One finds many of these in an unfinished state, or finished but broken at the perforation, obtained by making two conical holes which met and were then made into one cylindrical one. Where the axes are completely finished and unbroken, they are magnificent parade weapons or emblems of power. This is a logical interpretation in the case of some hammer-axes of beautifully perfect finish, corresponding to metal prototypes and stone imitations in central and southern Europe, and of which the Breton example from the Parc-Néhué, Riantec (Morbihan) Passage Grave shows a late Neolithic association.

The double or bipennate battle-axes are most frequently encountered. These may vary considerably in shape, but the Armorican specimens are almost all symmetrical, or nearly so. This gives a special character to the battle-axes of this region, and differentiates them from the Battle-axe cultures of eastern, central and northern Europe, where they are nearly all asymmetrical. The most perfect are boat-shaped, that is to say, their cutting edges are curved like the poop and prow of a canoe, and the upper and lower faces hollowed out like a skiff. Several of these objects have been found in Breton graves, in Late Neolithic contexts.

Plate 27

Fig. 18 Types of hammer-axes and battle-axes (bipennate or boat-shaped)

The Armorican polished axes are not made of rocks taken at random, and one must dismiss the legends which tell how Neolithic men, when they wished to make an axe, simply took a stone of approximately the right shape from the sea or the river and produced a finished object from it.[7] Only very tough and sound rocks are fit for such usage. If one makes a statistical survey of all the axes in public collections (nearly 3,500 for Brittany), 6 per cent are found to be made of various rocks and of imported flint in almost equal proportions; 70 per cent (more than the two-thirds) of the Breton polished axes are made of dolerite (including related greenstones), about 18 per cent of fibrolite and 5 per cent of rocks of the jadeite-eclogite group. (These figures exclude the axes of the Carnac mounds cultural group, which will be considered separately.)

THE MINING INDUSTRIES AND HANDICRAFTS

79

The distribution of the different types of axe may correspond to that of the rocks they are made of. Thus the concentration of axes in fibrolite (a massive variety of sillimanite) increases round the gulf of Morbihan, the bay of Audierne, the Bas-Léon and in the neighbourhood of Saint-Malo, where there are crystalline schists with sillimanite. In particular the outcrop of Port-Navalo, Arzon, at the entrance to the Morbihan gulf, must have supplied material for the veritable workshop which exis-ted in the island of Er-Lannic, where there are quantities of rough-outs and portable polishers. A small menhir, belonging to the alignment of Lannoulouarn, Plouguin (Finistère), had been used as a polisher, near another outcrop of fibrolite.

A complete petrographic study of the raw material of a sufficient quantity of polished axes (more than 500 have now been sliced in Armorica), by removing a fragment large enough to grind a thin section for examination under the petrological microscope, yields information of the utmost importance con-cerning the origin of the materials and the commerce in the finished products. However, there still remains the problem of the source of objects made of greenstone 'de luxe' rocks of the continuous series jadeite-chloromelanite-eclogite; although small dykes of these rocks which could have provided the material for some of the items (especially those of eclogite) have been found in Brittany, this does not exclude the probability of an Alpine (more specifically, a Piedmontese) origin for many of the handsome large jadeite axes found not only in the Carnac big mounds but also (with some variants of form, it is true) throughout western Europe, from Scotland to the Mediter-ranean. It should be noted, moreover, that the serpentine of the ring-discs, which form part of the same cultural ensemble as the fine ceremonial axes of these choice greenstone rocks, is often certainly Alpine in origin.

But if we turn to the immense series of axes made of doleritic rocks, we find that a petrographic study enables us to divide them into groups, the axes in each group being made of absolutely identical material. Thus the majority of Breton axes belong to group A, and specimens from this group, are found exported to England, the Channel Islands, Normandy, the Paris basin, and even as far as Alsace, then Touraine, Gascony, Saintonge, Poitou, Anjou and Maine. This group can be identified by virtue of certain characteristic features; these are the particular disposition of the inclusions of ilmenite, clustered together in short threads, the different threads running in various directions, and an extremely fine grain. Sometimes these features can be seen with the naked eye, on perfectly polished objects with a slight patina. Unfortunately, in spite of intensive research in the field, it has not yet been possible to find the corresponding outcrop (which must be unique), nor, therefore, any trace of a workshop, if there was one. Not only are most axes of the usual shapes made of dolerite of the A group (examples of these have already been met with in monuments attributed to the earlier Neolithic culture), but this material has also served for the manufacture of some perforated hammers and some fine boatshaped battleaxes. There is, too, a series of ceremonial axes made exclusively of group A dolerite. These are the button axes, objects of classical Armorican shape with a long butt, ending in a knob instead of a point.

Plate 26

Group C is of special interest. The rock is an ultrabasic greenstone, an unusual polymetamorphic hornblendite identical with an outcrop of rock at Kerlevot, Pleuven (Finistère). This material has been used for making only one ordinary axe, but a large series of battleaxes, often boatshaped, distributed beyond Brittany into Vendée and Normandy, as well as into the Seine and Loire basins, and even into Holland, where their distribution corresponds with the valleys (battleaxes have often been dredged from the beds of rivers). In Brittany these objects (either in the roughout state or completely finished) are particularly numerous on the south coast; half a dozen were found in

Plate 27
Fig. 19

F

graves of the Bigouden region (Finistère)—near the outcrop, therefore—in Late Neolithic contexts.[8]

Taking into consideration the very large number of objects, especially of group A, representing tons of material scattered over an immense area, one must envisage something very different from a limited barter system of commerce between near neighbours and much closer to an organised system of distribution to the consumers. Quarrying and the pecking or sawing of at least the rough shapes must therefore have been carried out on a scale almost amounting to an industry, which would imply the existence of specialist proletarian workers, whether slaves, serfs or 'paid' employees. Here one again encounters the same sort of sociological problems set by the erection of the megaliths themselves. As for the final transformation into a finished object, this could often have been carried out at consumer level. However, the existence of ranges of articles of standardised shape (button axes of group A dolerite; battleaxes, perhaps somewhat polymorphous at first sight but certainly from a single workshop, of group C hornblendite) and of workshops such as that at ErLannic, Arzon, which produced finished articles, not only of the local fibrolite, but also of group A dolerite (several hundred fragments of objects made of this material have been found there) suggests that this stage of manufacture was subject to some degree of organisation.

OCCUPATION AND FORTIFIED SITES

Apart from the graves and the goods found in them, we have little evidence concerning the Late Neolithic people. This is largely due to the fact that dwellings must have been essentially wooden structures which have a limited life, and which would leave no traces in the types of soils common in Armorica.

The only important occupation sites we know are fortified ones such as the camp at Lizo and the promontory site at CrohCollé, and traces on small islands—those of ErLannic and ErYoh. Moreover, there are serious difficulties in the way

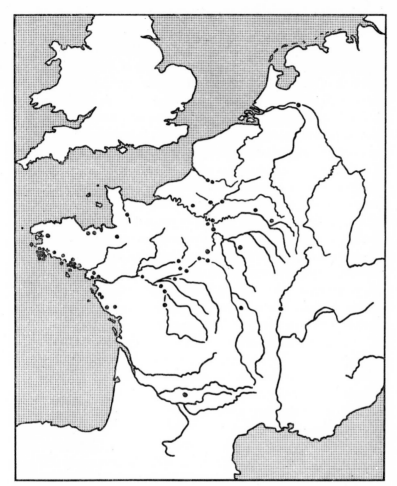

Fig. 19 Distribution map of battle-axes of Group C, made from hornblendite identical with outcrop at Kerlévot, Pleuven (F.), which is indicated by a cross

of dating these sites accurately; we are obliged, as in the case of tombs, to fall back on a typological study of the associated material, with all the lack of chronological precision that implies. It seems that some of these establishments may have begun with the first Neolithic culture; but their maximum utilisation was certainly during the Late Neolithic.

The camp of Lizo is situated near Carnac (Morbihan), on a rocky crest on the west bank of the Crach river.[9] It is about 200 m. long from north to south, and about 155 m. wide towards the southern end; it is surrounded by several embankments. The first of these follows the circumference of the crest; it is smaller where the steep slopes towards the river form a natural defence. Its other stretches are reinforced with a second ditch, outside and below it. An east-west earth-bank divides the interior of the camp into two. Roughly in the centre is a Passage Grave which has produced an interesting collection of material, comprising Chalcolithic and Neolithic cultural elements. The camp has a whole has not been thoroughly examined; the excavators certainly identified hut floors, semicircular ovens set in the embankments, and small mounds with cists containing charcoal, burnt earth, fragments of pottery and flint implements. Unfortunately, it is now impossible to re-establish exactly in which structure any of the articles were found; this would have helped to date the buildings concerned more precisely, since the camp as a whole seems also to have produced a great deal of Iron Age pottery.

The embankments are fairly simply constructed; they are agglomerations of stones piled against an inner supporting wall of dry stones or juxtaposed blocks. The whole erection may have been covered with a layer of earth. The hut foundations are indicated by walls formed of fairly large blocks laid flat. Several rooms of various shapes can be distinguished, some adjoining one another, and measuring up to 4·5 by 3 m. The ovens are set in the walls of the embankment, particularly in the north part of the camp. They are made of vertical blocks and roofed with oversailing flat slabs. The small mounds are also in the north part of the camp. The largest are 8 m. across. They are mostly circular, bounded by several blocks, and contain hearths and small cists.

This site is bestrewn with both hammerstones and querns. Nearly everywhere—around the ovens, in the mounds, in the hut foundations—a great many fragments of pots and large numbers of stone implements have been found. The pottery is almost all broken; fragments of coarse round-bottomed pots with incised decoration of the Conguel type, pieces of carinated bowls, fragments with pimple decoration in relief, knob lugs and a few rare pieces of beakers. In addition to numerous axes of dolerite, fibrolite and flint, the stone material consists of a great quantity of flint implements—blades, scrapers, awls, transverse arrows, almond-shaped arrows, arrows with concave base, tanged arrows, barbed and tanged arrows.

This settlement at Lizo, therefore, must have been of considerable importance. It was well fortified and well organised. The pottery is on the whole of a late type; moreover, to judge by the material found there, it is very probable that the Passage Grave was earlier than the encampment, and was included in the site accidentally.

The settlement at Croh-Collé, Saint-Pierre-Quiberon (Morbihan), is more or less similar, but it is by the sea, on the Côte Sauvage. It is on a rocky promontory, whose landward side was protected by a bank faced on either side with small vertical slabs. In the interior of the spur were hut foundations and a small megalithic tomb. The material found in the enclosure is clearly Late Neolithic; heavy 'flower-pot' ware and coarse round-bottomed pots with incised decoration or pimples in relief, dolerite axes, spindle whorls, barbed and tanged arrows, querns and hammerstones.

The islet of Er-Yoh is a rocky mass linked nowadays to the island of Houat (Morbihan) by a low causeway.[5] It is 80 m. long and 30 m. wide, and is dominated by two rocky peaks whose summit is 16 m. above sea level. Between these two peaks is a platform covered with sandy earth, where have been found hearths outlined with stones laid on edge. The latter have been in contact with fire, and there are traces of charred wood around them. In some places the sandy earth has been levelled and covered with fairly even paving. Habitations have been built over this flooring, with thick walls consisting of blocks laid flat. There is kitchen debris everywhere around, made up of all kinds of shellfish, fragments of the bones of domestic and wild animals (seals, beavers), jaws and bones of fish, and the bones of birds. Amongst this debris have been found fragments of coarse pottery—some with incised decoration—polished dolerite axes, awls, scrapers, numerous arrow-heads—especially tanged and barbed—and beads. Scattered amongst the hearths and dwellings have been found axes, cores, strikers and querns. Thanks to the nature of the soil, bone implements have also been preserved: awls, antler axe-handles, tool-handles and whistles.

The site of Er-Lannic, Arzon,[3] is quite different. This is a little island in the gulf of Morbihan; at the southern end of it are two circles of standing stones, touching one another. Near the foot of the standing stones belonging to the circle which is still half visible, above the sea and slightly further from it, hearths and cists have been found. In addition, the islet must have been covered with huts, and a considerable quantity of material has been recovered from them. A few fragments of pottery with pimples in relief and true channeled decoration can no doubt be classified as true Neolithic, perhaps a little retarded. There are other items belonging to the Chalcolithic culture: fragments of beakers, and a bone button with perfo-rated shank. Most of the pottery is Late Neolithic: fragments of coarse ware, some with incised decoration in the Conguel style, and then the series of fragments of vase-supports. The flint material is relatively plentiful; more than 15,000 flakes have been counted in the part that has been excavated, more than one-third of them retouched. Typical implements include: about 80 transverse arrows of all sizes, triangular, trapezoidal and scalene; about 20 barbed and tanged arrows of all shapes; two large triangular arrows; numerous awls, end-blade and circular scrapers, a flint axe, some dolerite axes, many of them broken, and part of an arc-pendant. Noteworthy is the abundance of fibrolite, in the shape of little flat axes, whole or fragmentary—an abundance connected with the nearness of the Port-Navalo outcrop. The site must, however, have been a veritable polishing workshop, to judge from the numbers of portable polishers found there.

In fact, many of these living-sites were occupied more or less uninterruptedly for a fairly long period; one therefore quite frequently finds objects in them dating from the Bronze and Iron Ages, the Gallo-Roman period, and even the Middle Ages.

In spite of the introduction and spread of a new type of megalithic tomb, the Gallery Grave, the Late Neolithic popu-lations continued to use Passage Graves of simple types fairly generally, but especially in the Atlantic zone. It is even possible that they continued to build this type of monument for a while. However, more complex types soon began to make their appearance, evolved from the simple Passage Grave.

LATE
NEOLITHIC
GRAVES

The re-utilisation of the earliest Passage Graves was very common. Some of these numerous graves have been found to contain Late Neolithic objects as well as articles of the true Neolithic culture. Examples of this are too numerous for us to name them all; it will suffice to mention the particularly heterogeneous grave-goods in the Kercado Passage Grave, Carnac (Morbihan). As well as Chalcolithic elements (Beaker pottery and gold plaques) this contained Neolithic round-bottomed pots, barbed and tanged arrow-heads, pendants,

EVOLUTION
OF THE
PASSAGE
GRAVES

callaïs beads, incised pottery, fragments of 'flower-pot' vessels, and axes of dolerite and jadeite. This monument, therefore, like many others, certainly continued in use till the beginning of the Bronze Age, if we accept the callaïs beads and jadeite axes in the Passage Graves as contemporaneous with those in the large Carnac mounds. This last point seems to be confirmed by the presence in one of the small Passage Graves (No. 2) of Parc-Guren, Crach (Morbihan), of a segmented faience bead, originating in Egypt (no doubt at Tel-el-Amarna) and an article of trade in about 1400 B.C., which brings us to the Early Bronze Age. Moreover, some Passage Graves were re-used in the Iron Age and the Gallo-Roman period; but early excava-tors did not always distinguish between the various super-imposed layers because the Gallo-Roman material often infil-trated into the lower layers.

Even as regards the purely Neolithic material, excavators rarely paid much attention to possible stratigraphical evidence. It is true that the objects were usually dispersed and mixed, and it is difficult to determine in what order the various elements arrived. However, in some of the Morbihan Passage Graves (Port-Blanc, Saint-Pierre-Quiberon; Conguel, Quiberon; and Kervilor, La-Trinité-sur-Mer) two levels of filling have been identified; the first rests on a lower paving, and bears a second paving above which is a second filling. These monu-ments in fact present cases of subdivisions of one single level, without any further refinement, though it is alleged that at Con-guel only incised ware was found in the lower level, and only Beakers in the upper one.[10] The stratigraphy observed in Passage Grave D of Barnenez, Plouézoc'h (Finistère), shows very clearly the re-utilisation of the monument by the latest Neolithic culture.[11] In Passage Grave C, some obviously late fragments have suggested that the tomb was in use for a fairly long period. The lower level of Passage Grave D corresponds with what is found in the other graves of the Barnenez cairn, and is definitely true Neolithic (already with additional Chalcolithic elements); the upper level, a bed of large stones laid deliberately and scattered throughout the passage and the chamber, contains large fragments of coarse pottery ('flowerpots'), three dolerite axes, and an axe of unpolished flint.

It is reasonable to wonder whether some Passage Graves were not built in Late Neolithic times. There are indeed some that have produced exclusively Late Neolithic material; one of these is the Tossen-ar-Run Passage Grave, Yvias,[12] which is a corbelled monument, still under its barrow, and which has only produced pottery of a coarse type. But it is also possible that this monument was built in the Early Neolithic and yet was not furnished with material of that culture, as was the case, for example, with some of the Passage Graves of Barnenez, Plouézoc'h.

What is more certain is that the Passage Graves underwent a definite evolution in two different directions: on the one hand, side chambers were added; on the other, a definite angle or bend was given to some monuments.

The Passage Graves with side chambers no doubt originated in the Passage Graves with a rectangular or sub-rectangular chamber. The side chambers came to be grafted either on to the chamber or on to the passage. One of the most interesting examples illustrating the genesis of these graves is probably that provided by the three Passage Graves in a single barrow at Rondossec, Plouharnel (Morbihan). All three have the same orientation, and are monuments with a long passage; two have a definitely rectangular chamber. The third has a rectangular chamber shorter than those of the other two, but with a little cell opening off one side of it. One of the Passage Graves at Mané-Bras, Erdeven, and that at Kermarker, La-Trinité-sur-Mer are on the same plan. The Passage Grave of Loqueltas, Locoal-Mendon (Morbihan) is identical except that it has two

Fig. 20

Fig. 21

side chambers, one on either side of the main chamber. In the east monument at Les-Mousseaux, Pornic (Loire-Atlantique), a P-shaped Passage Grave with a long passage, it is this part that has a little side chamber. These side chambers are some-times more numerous; at Mané-Groh, Erdeven (Morbihan) there are four leading off the main chamber.[13]

As in the case of the simple Passage Graves, the inner height increases from the passage entrance up to the chamber. The side chambers are roofed in a somewhat special way; each is covered by a slab, and the stone table covering the central chamber sometimes rests on these. The barrow is round or slightly oval, never long like the barrows of Gallery Graves.

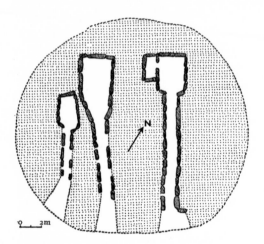

Fig. 20 Plan of the barrow of Rondossec, Plouharnel (M.), containing three Passage Graves, one with a side-chamber

The distribution of these graves is significant; in Armorica they are found only on the southern coast. They never occur in zones where the Gallery Graves abound (Côtes-du-Nord; north and inner Finistère), but are situated in the areas where Passage Graves are plentiful, i.e. the coast of Loire-Atlantique, the Carnac region and the Bigouden area.

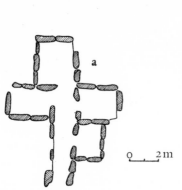

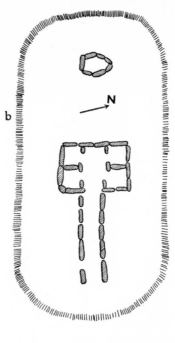

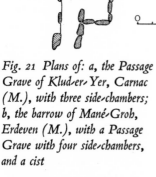

Fig. 21 Plans of: a, the Passage
Grave of Klud-er-Yer, Carnac
(M.), with three side-chambers;
b, the barrow of Mané-Groh,
Erdeven (M.), with a Passage
Grave with four side-chambers,
and a cist

The angled monuments may be the culmination of the uni-
lateral development of the chamber of a Passage Grave, at right
angles to the passage or at an obtuse angle. The monument is
always wider towards the distal end; the inner height is also
definitely greater in the terminal section than at the entrance of
the passage. At Les Pierres-Plates, Locmariaquer (Morbihan),
a little chamber is formed at the end by a transveral orthostat;
the same monument also has a small lateral cell at the bend.
These angled monuments have a round barrow, fairly high,
completely covering the Passage Grave. The barrows of Le-
Rocher, Le Bono (Morbihan), and of Poulguen, Penmarch
(Finistère) are particularly fine.

Fig. 22

There are only a few tombs of this type; about half a dozen
in the Morbihan region (Locoal-Mendon, Carnac, Bono,

Crach, Locmariaquer), and two in southern Finistère, including the monument of RunAour, Plomeur, which is slightly different: it had a fine circular drywalled chamber, now destroyed, into which led two converging passages built with large slabs (reconstructed alongside the Musée Préhistorique

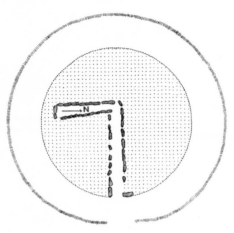

Fig. 22 Plan of the barrow of Le Rocher, Le Bono (M.), covering a Passage Grave with long angled passage. $\frac{1}{500}$

Finistérien). In any case, the distribution remains the same as that of the Passage Graves with side chambers, i.e., strictly in the south of Brittany.

This series of angled monuments is also interesting for another reason: it possesses a series of rather special carvings, of which those of Luffang, Crach (Morbihan), and of LesPierresPlates at Locmariaquer are widely known. As always, the interpretation of these motifs is a very delicate matter, and many writers have indulged in rash speculations as to their meaning. There are some who take them to represent a cephalopod (in particular, the figure known as the 'octopus' at Luffang) with its eyes and tentacles, others consider them to be stylisations of

Plate 31
Plate 30

the human body. In actual fact, the figures are sub-rectangular carvings, usually symmetrical, and decorated with circles arranged on either side of a central axis. Sometimes there is a 'head' surmounting the rectangle. In one example the circles are replaced by oblique lines placed like the veins in a frond of bracken.

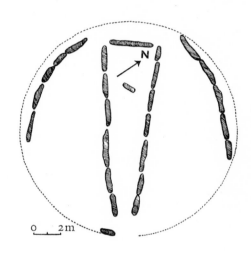

Fig. 23 Plan of the Passage Grave of Ty-ar-Boudiquet, Brennilis (F.), with kerbstones

Other interesting problems are set by one of the finest of the monuments, Ty-ar-Boudiquet, Brennilis (Finistère), which is probably of a late period. It is unquestionably a Passage Grave —a somewhat unusual one, certainly, since there is not a very clear differentiation between the passage and the chamber. The passage, which is narrow, merges imperceptibly into a long trapezoidal chamber, very wide at the far end. The barrow was probably sub-circular, and surrounded by a partial kerb not unlike that of the Gallery Graves, built of fairly large blocks of stone laid on edge—rather unusual around a Passage Grave. The most surprising feature of this monument is its geographi-

Fig. 23

cal position, right in the centre of the region and completely isolated from the coastal Passage Graves. There are no grave-goods to give us a relative date for this tomb. Some authorities consider it to be a transitional form between Passage Grave and the Gallery Grave, but there does not seem to be any other evidence to support this theory.

THE TOMBS OF THE LOIRE TYPE In the north-east part of Morbihan and in Ille-et-Vilaine there are three monuments which can be linked with the Loire valley type of megalithic edifice (Touraine and Anjou), such as that of Bagneux (Maine-et-Loire).[14] This type is charac-terised by its great size; it has a very long chamber, which is also very wide and high, and is preceded by a short very low passage.

Fig. 24
Plate 32

The finest of these three sites is that of La-Roche-aux-Fées, Essé (Ille-et-Vilaine). It is about $19\frac{1}{2}$ m. long, and consists of a monumental entry opening into a little passage $3\frac{1}{2}$ m. long, 3 m. wide, and only just over 1 m. high. Two orthostats at right angles to the axle of the monument divide the passage from the chamber, which is very large and divided into four by three septal pillars. The whole chamber is 14 m. long, its average width is 4 m., and the ceiling is about 2 m. high. The whole construction is covered by eight enormous capstones. Capstones and supports are of red Cambrian schist; the nearest outcrop of this rock is over 4 km. away. Each slab weighs 40 to 45 metric tons; this is the biggest transport undertaking for which we have evidence in Armorica.

La Tablette, Cournon (Morbihan), is part of a vast monu-ment in the same style as the Roche-aux-Fées. The Maison-Trouvée at La-Ville-au-Voyer, La-Chapelle (Morbihan), is a megalithic tomb comprising a short passage 1·2 m. wide, and a chamber $4\frac{1}{2}$ by $2\frac{1}{2}$ m. In this series of large monuments, no grave-goods have ever been found, and one is therefore justified in wondering whether they are graves or temples.

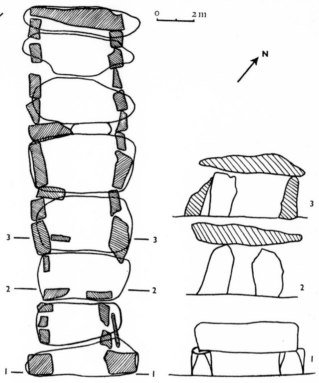

Fig. 24 Plan of the Roche-aux-Fées, Essé (I.-et-V.)

The cists, either isolated or in groups, which are found in great numbers in southern Finistère (between Pointe-du-Raz and the Odet) and in Morbihan (especially in the Quiberon peninsula) are very definitely graves. Since many of them are in ground favourable to the preservation of bones, skeletons of children or adults are sometimes found in them; these are lying on their sides in a contracted position, the knees drawn up towards the chin.

The finest cists are enclosed by six slabs; four laid on edge, one forming the 'floor', and the last serving as a cover. The

THE LATE
LONG
MOUNDS
AND
THE STONE
CISTS

95

stones are usually very skilfully fitted together. The length of these cists varies between 80 and 160 cm., their width and depth between 40 and 60 cm.

Some of those on the Quiberon peninsula are much smaller, being 40 cm. long and 20 cm. wide. Not all these tombs are equally well constructed; many are built of roughly laid stones, and have no covering.

Sometimes several cists are grouped together in small cemeteries, known as mounds when they are covered by a little barrow. Such mounds are, of course, not connected with the long-mounds of the initial Neolithic culture. They have no precise structure. At Parc-ar-Hastel, Tréguennec (Finistère), the cists are encased in a framework of stones, itself covered with a layer of clay. The cemetery on the island of Thinic, Saint-Pierre-Quiberon (Morbihan), is simply covered with a shapeless heap of large stones. The mound at Parc-ar-Hastel (one of the finest) is roughly circular (35 to 40 m. in diameter), and 2 m. high. It contains three types of tombs: fine cists constructed with 5 or 6 slabs (where there is no bottom block the floor is covered with a bed of sand or shells), graves enclosed by irregular blocks, and roughly constructed cists without a covering.

The goods found in or around these graves can be ascribed to the Late Neolithic culture. They consist of coarse pottery (on the island of Thinic fragments have been found with incised and *pointillé* decoration), flint flakes, scrapers, pendants, polished axes and even battle axes (a cist at Botvélec, Pont-l'Abbé, Finistère, has produced two boat-shaped double axes, and the handsome boat-axe of hornblendite from Mané-Meur, Quiberon, Morbihan, is from a cist included in the barrow of a small Passage Grave), strikers and crushers.

However, it would be inaccurate to attribute all the cists to the Late Neolithic cultures. This type of grave occurs again at a still later epoch—in the Bronze Age, and even in the Iron

Age. It is therefore impossible to give any precise date for those cists which have not yielded any grave-goods.

On the south coast of Finistère, between the mouths of the Odet and the Audierne river, there are numerous graves grouped into cemeteries which are often very large. The damage inflicted on them by quarrying has made it difficult to study them. These burial grounds comprise numerous juxtaposed monuments—cists, simple Passage Graves, or Passage Graves with side chambers. These various tombs are either isolated, each having its own barrow, or grouped within a single mound, and it is often far from easy to separate the various juxtaposed elements.

The largest group is that at Lesconil, Plobannalec (Finistère). Although it has now totally disappeared, it is one of the best known, because it was relatively well excavated.[15] It consisted of about ten small barrows, covering either a simple cist, or several cists, or a sort of Passage Grave with small lateral chambers or cells; in addition, there was a fine Passage Grave in the midst of the site. The grave-goods found there consist of coarse pottery (large 'flower-pots' with knob handles, and bowls with rounded base), blades of 'Grand-Pressigny' flint, pendants and spindle-whorls, polished axes including two double axes (one boat-shaped, of hornblendite), and a handsome Western dagger of copper. These goods show that the cemetery was widely used by the people of the Late Neolithic culture and up to the Bronze Age, since in the chamber of the Passage Grave were found two flanged axes, one flat chisel-shaped axe, and eight space-plates of amber, similar to those from Early Bronze Age barrows. At Treffiagat (Finistère), several cemeteries of this kind have yielded goods of a fairly late date, including coarse round-bottomed pots, pendants and polished axes.

At Plouhinec (Finistère), on the plateau of Le Souc'h, chambers, galleries and cists are linked together very irregularly.

G

The furniture includes numerous Late Neolithic objects: 'flower-pots', coarse round-bottomed pots, arc-pendants, ordinary pendants, tanged arrows and polished axes. However, articles definitely belonging to an earlier period were also found; in particular, small round-bottomed pots, some in the shape of leather bottles, with handles perforated subcutaneously, typical of the first Neolithic culture.

It is possible that these complex burial grounds grew up around a first grave whose antiquity is vouched for by the presence of objects from the Early Neolithic culture. Small cists were added, one after another, and also debased Passage Graves with side chambers, of a late type. But the greatest development took place with the Late Neolithic culture. These cemeteries were certainly in use till the Bronze Age. In some of them articles from the Iron Age have been found here and there (in particular, at Le Souc'h); this indicates a reversion to the site and not uninterrupted use.

THE
GALLERY
GRAVES

While Passage Graves continued to be used, and were modified with varying degrees of complexity a new type of grave was developing throughout Armorica: the Gallery Grave. From the typological point of view, these are entirely different from the Passage Graves, and represent a new mega-lithic phase. Their grave-goods, unlike those of the Passage Graves, are very homogeneous, and belong exclusively to the Late Neolithic cultures with sometimes some Chalcolithic material.[16]

Plate 33, 34

The typical Gallery Grave is a monument consisting of two straight parallel lines of orthostats, on which rest covering slabs. If both ends are closed by blocks of stone, the result is a

Fig. 25a

very long cist (Kermeur-Bihan, Moëlan, Finistère); but this is very rarely the case. The more frequent and more normal type is in the form of a very long 'corridor', with an entrance at one

Fig. 25c

side and a closing slab at the other end (Trédaniel, Côtes-du-

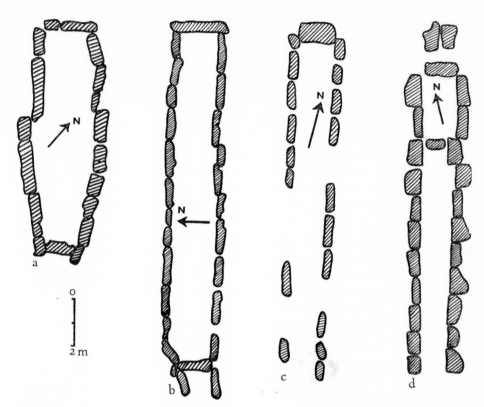

Fig. 25 Plans of the Gallery Graves of: a, Kermeur-Bihan, Moëlan (F.); b, Kerandrèze, Moëlan (F.); c, Trédaniel (C.-du-N.); d, La-Ville-au-Bourg, Rouillac (C.-du-N.)

Nord). Either way, these monuments are always narrow (about 120 to 140 cm.), with low ceilings, and have no distinct chamber higher or wider than the 'corridor'.

Gallery Graves are often divided in two unequal parts by a transverse orthostat; this forms a short 'cella' on one side, and a long 'antechamber' on the other (Le Net, at Saint-Gildas-de-Rhuis, Morbihan). In no instance, of course, is the 'cella'

Plate 35

99

wider or higher than the antechamber; no comparison can therefore be made with the Passage Grave structures. Sometimes there is a short vestibule at the entrance, not formed by any modification of the width of the gallery, but by a division consisting of a transverse orthostat with a notch or a piece cut out. At Saint-Servais (Côtes-du-Nord), on the edge of the forest of Duault, the Gallery Grave of Toul-an-Urz has an enormous notched orthostat, providing a kennel-hole entrance. One of the three Gallery Graves on the heathland of Liscuis at Laniscat (Côtes-du-Nord) also has a kennel-hole, smaller, but of similar construction.

Fig. 27a

The position of the entrance varies. Normally it is axial, but in some cases it is lateral, and may then be preceded by a little vestibule (Coët-Correc, Mur-de-Bretagne, Côtes-du-Nord). As in the case of Gallery Graves with an axial entrance, the lateral vestibule may be separated from the gallery itself by stone blocks with pieces hollowed out, a pair of which form a port-hole. Some Gallery Graves have a lateral port-hole with no vestibule—but the latter may have disappeared (Kerléarec, Carnac, Morbihan).

Fig. 26b

The Gallery Grave of Mélus, near Loguivy-de-la-Mer, Ploubazlanec (Côtes-du-Nord), shows a variation: the entrance is a lateral one, beneath a lintel, and the lateral vestibule is simulated by two small stones. At Kerlescan, Carnac (Morbihan), there were two port-holes; one, on one side, in the orthostats of the gallery, and the other in blocks which divided the monument into two parts.

Fig. 27b

Some Gallery Graves have a second row of orthostats alongside the main ones, perhaps for reinforcement. It is surprising, however, to find that this always exists only on one side of the tomb (La-Ville-Gesnouan, Créhen, Côtes-du-Nord). More frequently, one finds a kerb, or the remains of one, at varying distances from the monument and completely surrounding it. In some cases it marks the extent of the construction mound

Fig. 29

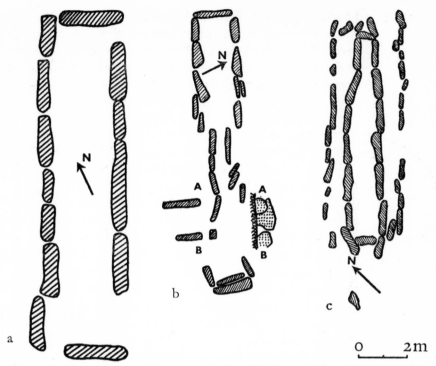

Fig. 26 Plans of the Gallery Graves of: a, Kervéret, Plounévez-Loc'hrist (F.); b, Coët-Correc, Mur-de-Bretagne (C.-du-N.), with lateral entrance and port-hole; c, Lesconil, Poullan (F.), with buttressed orthostats and kerbstones

(Liscuis, Laniscat, Côtes-du-Nord); in others, it holds up the earth of the mound, preventing the main orthostats from being forced outwards. In the latter case, the stones of the kerb may be fairly close to the orthostats of the gallery (L'Ile-Grande, Pleumeur-Bodou, Côtes-du-Nord). The stones of the kerb vary in size; at L'Ile-Grande they are fairly large, while those at Liscuis are very small.

The *arc-bouté* Gallery Graves represent a simpler type. Only three of these exist, all in southern Finistère (Lesconil,

Fig. 26

Plate 38

Plate 37

Poullan; Castel-Ruffel near Saint-Goazec; and Goulet-Riec, Riec-sur-Belon). These are distinguished by the absence of covering slabs, the two parallel lines of orthostats being propped so that the stones of one row support those of the other. Of course, this does not mean that they lack the classic architectural

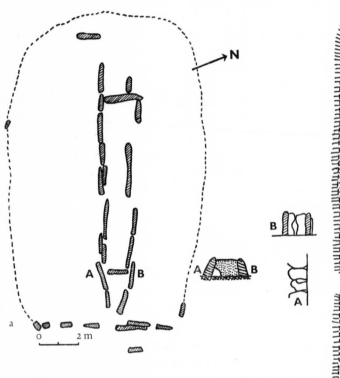

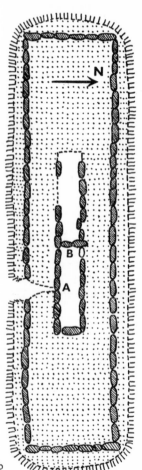

Fig. 27 Plans of: a, one of the Gallery Graves of Liscuis, Laniscat (C.-du-N.); b, the Gallery Grave of Kerlescan, Carnac (M.), with kerbstones and two series of notched orthostats

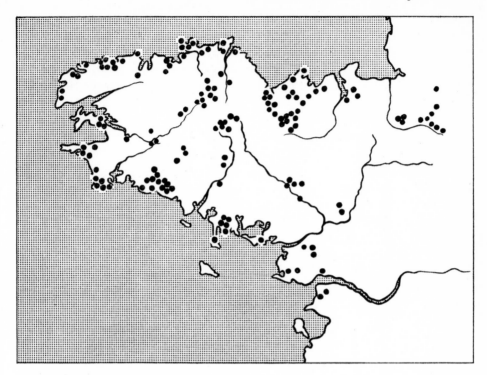

Fig. 28 Distribution map of Gallery Graves

details; Lesconil, Poullan, for example, has a little 'cella' and a very fine kerb.

Like the Passage Graves, most of the Gallery Graves must have had a fairly flat paving. It is always found in properly excavated monuments. This is an important detail, showing that the builders were concerned with improving the interior aspect of the tomb. For the same reason, the orthostats and the covering slabs have their flat sides turned inwards—the sides, that is to say, resulting from the splitting or cleavage of the stone blocks.

Fig. 28

The general distribution of the Gallery Graves differs to a marked degree from that of the Passage Graves. The latter are only found spread along the Armorican littoral, with fairly large concentrations at some points; the Gallery Graves, on the other hand, are scattered more or less everywhere, in the interior as well as along the coast. Moreover, they are hardly ever found in large groups; very occasionally, two or three occur near each other, but usually there is only one to a *commune*. All the same, in spite of this general dispersal, some districts are more favoured than others, especially the Côtes-du-Nord and Finistère. This fact is easily explained by the abundance in these areas of material suitable for megalithic building. The Rennes basin, for example, whose substratum consists of schist entirely useless for the production of massive blocks, is without any megalithic monuments. Furthermore, in regions where Passage Graves are numerous (Morbihan, the peninsula of Penmarch, and that of Crozon, in Finistère), Gallery Graves are comparatively rare.

From the topographical point of view, the Gallery Graves are also found in more varied locations than the Passage Graves. They occupy all kinds of positions—on hill-tops (like those on the heathlands of Liscuis, Laniscat, for example), on slopes, or even at the bottom of depressions, like that of Men-Guionnet, Gourin (Morbihan). There are even some, built in low-lying situations not far from the sea, which are now on the foreshore, regularly covered by the incoming tide (Lerret, Kerlouan, and Kornig, Plouescat, Finistère). This is one of the many proofs of the rise of sea-level since the Pleistocene period.

The fact that these tombs are widely distributed is certainly the chief factor responsible for the variation in their general appearance, the material used depending upon what was available on the site. Now, rocks do not all split up in the same way. Dolerites, granodiorites, phtanites, produce enormous squat, shapeless blocks, and a megalith built of them has a massive

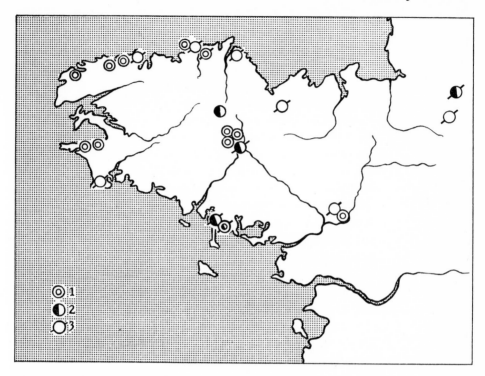

Fig. 29 Distribution map of Gallery Graves of particular types: 1, with kerbstones; 2, with kennel-holes; 3, with lateral entrance. The superposition of the different signs indicates the simultaneous possession of these different characteristics

appearance. The monuments round the bay of Saint-Brieuc (Côtes-du-Nord) are of this type.

In southern Finistère, on the other hand, particularly in the neighbourhood of the Aven valley, the migmatite rocks belonging to the metamorphic series of South Cornouaille have produced thin, flat orthostats and broad capstones. Three of these stones suffice to cover a Gallery Grave 13 m. long, like that of Coat-Luzuen, Melgven (Finistère). In the centre of Brittany, at Laniscat and at Mur-de-Bretagne (Côtes-du-Nord) schist has been used—a more easily worked material, permitting more regular construction.

There is no known example in Armorica of a Gallery Grave covered with a barrow; one only finds, in some cases, a construction mound reaching at the most to the height of the top of the orthostats. The mound was needed for setting the capstones in position. Very frequently, the construction mound has now entirely disappeared, the earth having been removed for agricultural purposes. It is also possible that the slabs were rolled up or down wooden ramps, which, of course, have also disappeared.

A large number of Gallery Graves were already empty when first discovered—violated, no doubt, a very long time ago. They would have been an easier prey than the Passage Graves, which were protected by a massive barrow. We therefore know absolutely nothing about the grave-goods of these tombs in the interior of Brittany, nor of most of those in the east of Côtes-du-Nord and in Ille-et-Vilaine. The Gallery Graves which have preserved their original filling compensate for this to some degree; they have often produced abundant and interesting material.

The grave-goods found in them consist essentially of Late Neolithic objects such as those already described: 'flower-pots', coarse bowls and dishes, carinated pots, so-called 'collared flasks', daggers and knives of honey-coloured flint, polished axes, arrows and pendants. Chalcolithic elements are not infrequent: Beaker ware, daggers of arsenical copper, bone buttons, archers' wrist-guards. This association of Neolithic and Chalcolithic elements is not universal; some monuments, such as that of Mélus, Ploubazlanec (Côtes-du-Nord), contained no Chalcolithic objects. On the other hand, the Gallery Grave of Kerbors (Côtes-du-Nord) produced goods which were almost exclusively Chalcolithic, but with Beaker ware of local origin made according to Late Neolithic techniques.

A few rare and exceptional objects should also be men‐
tioned: a long‐tanged dagger at Tertre‐de‐l'Eglise, Plévenon
(Côtes‐du‐Nord), about which we unfortunately know very
little for certain, but which may be related to the so‐called
'Cypriot' daggers (see *infra*); and some amber beads, including
an oval one at Trédaniel and several at Krec'h‐Bleiz, Penvénan
(Côtes‐du‐Nord).

The engraving and sculpture found on some of the Gallery
Graves are noticeably different from the Passage Grave
engravings. Only four Gallery Graves possess decorations:
Mougau‐Bihan, Commana (Finistère), Prajou‐Menhir, Tré‐
beurden (Côtes‐du‐Nord), Kergüntuil, Trégastel (Côtes‐du‐
Nord), and Maison‐des‐Feins, Tressé (Ille‐et‐Vilaine).[17]

The motif found most frequently is sculptured breasts: these
are always in pairs, and two pairs are often grouped side by side
in a cartouche. No doubt these represent the 'Mother‐Goddess'
in a very simplified and symbolic form. Sometimes one can
make out a simple necklace below the breasts (Kergüntuil and
Prajou‐Menhir).

If the soul was assured of nourishment in the after‐life by this
representation of the Mother‐Goddess, it also required weapons
with which to defend itself. The axe with a handle is only
represented once, at Mougau‐Bihan, where the handle ends in
a curved butt. On the other hand, there are numerous repre‐
sentations of daggers, both at Mougau‐Bihan and at Prajou‐
Menhir. These are long‐bladed daggers, broad, with very dis‐
tinct lobes at the base. The tang is long, and sometimes curved
at the end. There are eight daggers of this type at Mougau‐
Bihan; at Prajou‐Menhir there are three—one isolated, the
other two together in a large panel, linked by double rows of
dots. These daggers seem to be copied from metal weapons
found throughout the eastern Mediterranean and Central
Europe, and often called 'Cypriot' daggers.

It is interesting to observe that at Prajou-Menhir and at Tressé the decorations are found only in the compartment or 'cella', indicating that this may perhaps be a sanctuary, isolated from the main tomb.

STATUE-
MENHIRS

The recent excavation of a curious barrow at Kermené, Guidel (Morbihan) has shown that there were also monuments of other types.[18] This barrow, in the shape of a truncated cone, contains no chamber or cist, but is built up of layers of earth with mixed-up heaps of sherds of Late Neolithic pottery, flints, a jadeite axe-head, an arc-pendant, charcoal and a few fragments of charred bones. It is covered by a similarly shaped revetment of stones, and set on an outer circle of larger blocks. Both in the revetment and in this base, one finds a huge quantity of broken querns, and amidst these, there are also three pieces of a broken statue-menhir.

This had a cone-shaped head, very regular, with a sort of crown; the top of the face is indicated by a ridge, but the rest of it is lost. The right-hand half of the torso shows the shoulder, and the fore-arm coming under the breast. The modelling of this stylised feminine statue, probably the Mother-Goddess, is very fine. It must be compared to the statue-menhirs of Guernsey, especially the Câtel one (that of Saint-Martin has been re-cut in the Iron Age, and given a face). These three Armorican figurations belong certainly to the same cultural context.

The Carnac Cultural Group

AMONG THE MANY MONUMENTS scattered over the Carnac region and the area around the gulf of Morbihan, a group of large mounds can be distinguished which are marked out both by their architecture and their furniture as forming an assemblage dating from the dawn of the Bronze Age.

The type example is a huge mound covering a central funerary chamber, without any passage leading into it, some-times accompanied by secondary cists. The principal monu-ments of this group are: at Carnac, Saint-Michel and Le Moustoir; at Locmariaquer, Mané-er-Hroeg, Er-Grah, Kerlud, Mané-Lud; and at Arzon, Tumiac (the Grand-Mont or Butte-de-César).

These large monuments were noticed quite early, and there are descriptions of them in works written before 1850; the en-thusiasm aroused by the first archaeological researches towards the middle of the last century led to organised excavations (Tumiac: 1853).[1]

Plate 36

These mounds are built on a fairly regular rectangular, trapezoidal or elliptical plan. Their length varies from 80 to 100 m., their width from 35 to 50 m. The average height is about 5 to 6 m., often varying in the same monument, when it has not been lowered to form a platform for a later building (chapel and calvary of Saint-Michel, Carnac).

ARCHI-TECTURE

The general structure is as follows: beneath the surface covering of stones is an intermediary layer of clay, then the central cairn enclosing the principal chamber. The monument is often built against a classic Passage Grave, which, as we shall see, seems to be earlier than the mound.

Of course, there are variations; at Saint-Michel, for example, there are retaining walls or facings east and west; at Mané-er-Hroeg the intermediary layer of clay is absent; at Er-Grah there is a peristalith, and at Mané-Lud a double row of small menhirs to the east of the monument, placed symmetrically in relation to the earlier large Passage Grave to the west, against which the tumulus is built.

The main chamber may be variously orientated, and is rarely the only one. It is usually accompanied by little secondary cists. The average dimensions of the chamber are about 4 by 2 m., and nearly 1 m. high. The walls are formed of blocks or bonded stones, but there is usually a clear differentiation between a well-built section and another part closed with sloping blocks, their upper end leaning against the covering slab. This last section of wall probably corresponds to the 'doorway' of the chamber, covered up after utilisation. At Tumiac one can even distinguish two parts: a megalithic chamber and a kind of narrower ante-chamber formed of dry stone walls supporting two small covering slabs. Uusually the chamber is covered with capstones, or with fairly short slabs slightly corbelled, as at Mané-Lud.

The chamber is sometimes hollowed out of the earth. It may have a paving, single or in two parts as at Mané-er-Hroeg. In some cases, traces of rotten wood have been found—possibly indicating a decayed floor (Tumiac, Mané-Lud).

Moustoir is exceptional, in that instead of a principal chamber, there is a large central hearth. However, the other characteristics of the monument—its irregular cists and its large bulk—clearly connect it with the series.

The cists may be fairly numerous; the excavators at Saint-Michel came upon about twenty of them.[2] They may appear to be absent (e.g. at Mané-er-Hroeg—a monument which in any case has not yet been completely excavated), but the restoration of Tumiac showed the existence of secondary cists near the central chamber, which was thought to be the only one. This may be the usual arrangement, therefore. These cists are fairly uneven; the smallest are often built of several stones leaning against each other (Saint-Michel).

The neighbouring or underlying Passage Graves seem to have no connexion with the main monuments, as can be seen from a study of their architecture and grave goods. At Saint-Michel the Passage Grave, with typical Western Neolithic furniture, is embedded in the outer layer of stones, almost outside the barrow. In the same way, the Passage Grave at Moustoir is not covered by the central cairn, but only by the intermediary layer of clay.

The polished axes from these tombs are the most famous of all, both because of the rare stones of which they are made and because of their shape, their finish or their unusual size—some are more than 45 cm. long. In some cases they have been found in great numbers: 106 at Mané-er-Hroeg, 39 at Saint-Michel, 30 at Tumiac. The breaking of several specimens may correspond to some ritual act. The materials used are essentially rocks of the fibrolite and jadeite (merging into eclogite) groups. The proportions are as follows: fibrolite 76 per cent, jadeite and eclogite 23 per cent. The abundance of fibrolite is connected with the proximity of the Port-Navalo outcrop, at Arzon.

GRAVE-GOODS

Fig. 30

The large axes are spindle-shaped in section, or, less frequently, sub-quadrangular. The finest of the Mané-er-Hroeg axes has a median rib, which makes the section almost lozenge-shaped. The butts are usually triangular, rarely rectangular, at least in this first group. The most remarkable feature is that some specimens have slightly splayed cutting edges in imitation of metal types. These models may be as much as 46·5 cm. long, and are fashioned from stone of the jadeite group. Others are similar in shape, but smaller (20 cm. or less); they are perforated near the heel, and may have been used as pendants.

Plate 41

Finally, the fibrolite axes are small, and their thin, rectangular form is reminiscent of the flat copper axes.

All these models, therefore, differ from the traditional Neolithic types. Their shape is strongly influenced by metal prototypes which must have existed. Polished stone objects may have been preferred for ceremonies of a funerary or religious nature, the earliest articles in metal being used for purely practical purposes.

The celebrated serpentine ring-disc of Mané-er-Hroeg is important because such objects of precious rock imported from the Alpine regions are most often found in hoards, or isolated without any accompanying objects. This is also the case with the fine ceremonial axes. Similar axes and serpentine or jadeite ring-discs have been found here and there throughout Armorica, where they were adopted by late Neolithic peoples; but finds are more frequent in the direction of Morbihan. Two hoards of very fine axes, from Bernon, Arzon, of 24 and 17 objects respectively, some perforated at the butt, should be noted in this connexion; also a find at Saint-Julien, Quiberon, consisting of 4 serpentine ring-discs and 2 jadeite axes.

Great quantities of callaïs were found in this group of mounds, where a total of 411 beads and pendants were recorded: Tumiac 249, Saint-Michel 136, Mané-er-Hroeg 49, Er-Grah 6. The pendants are pear-shaped, the perforations formed by the junction of two truncated cones. The beads are disc-shaped; no tubular ones were found, such as occur in some of the Passage Graves. It is difficult to know how the beads were worn; one of the engravings in the main chamber at Tumiac shows a necklace or gorget with several rows of beads.

In marked contrast to the wealth of polished axes and beads, the almost entire absence of flint and pottery is also typical of this cultural group. One may, however, mention a few fragments of Late Neolithic type found at Mané-Lud. The

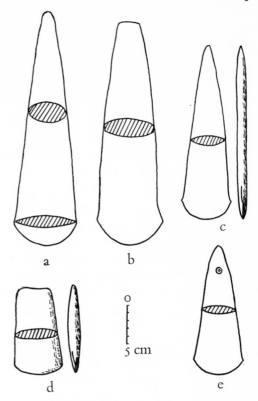

Fig. 30 Types of polished stone axes from the mounds of the Carnac group: a, from the Sarzeau hoard (M.); b, isolated find at the Sept-Saints, Erdeven (M.); c, mound of Saint-Michel, Carnac (M.); d and e, mound of Mané-er-Hroeg, Locmariaquer (M.). Apart from d which is of fibrolite, the axes are of greenstones of rare types of the group jadeite-chloromelanite-eclogite

Moustoir barrow, already unusual because of its large central hearth, has yielded up a large vase. The ware is thin and badly fired. The body of the vessel is 40 cm. in diameter; the base is rounded, and half-way up the vase is a little loop for suspension. Its profile is reminiscent of some forms of Western pottery; but its size recalls late Neolithic or Bronze Age specimens.

The chambers of these large mounds often contain a number of bones. The central hearth of Moustoir has produced bones caked together inextricably and difficult to identify; however, the teeth of horses have been recognised. The small cists of the

Saint-Michel mound have sometimes yielded bones of ruminants; during the restoration of Tumiac, the horn of a bovid was unearthed in the principal chamber. But it is again Mané-Lud which provides the most curious example: each pillar of the easternmost alignment supported a horse's skull. Animals evidently played an important part in funerary ceremonies. A few fragments of human bones have been found at Tumiac, Mané-Lud, Mané-er-Hroeg and Saint-Michel. In these monuments the bones seem to have been at least partly burnt before being placed in the funerary chambers.

In this particular group of monuments, called, for the sake of convenience, the Carnac group, one can already distinguish the architectural characteristics which were to be the general rule in Early Bronze Age barrows: a funerary chamber, sometimes hollowed out of the ground, closed and without any entrance passage, and sometimes with a wooden flooring.

As regards the grave-goods, the Neolithic tradition continues; but the existence at this period of metal objects is revealed by the new shapes adopted by those made of stone. The globular protuberances carved on some of the blocks at Tumiac may also be related to the representations of pairs of breasts belonging to the Gallery Grave culture.

The Carnac group of mounds no doubt developed parallel with the late Neolithic cultures and those of the Early Bronze Age. It is an example of a backward culture; but it may be noted that barrows containing four-handled pots made their appearance as far as Carnac itself, showing that by the beginning of the Middle Bronze Age the normal Bronze Age culture had reached the coastal regions of Morbihan, if indeed it had not infiltrated earlier.

The Menhirs and the Alignments

THE STANDING STONES, whose popular Breton names are *menhir* or *peulvan* (the former established by scientific usage) are characteristic elements of the classic Breton land-scape. They are to be found in many western European coun-tries, and even in Central Europe, but nowhere else do they occur so frequently, either singly or in imposing groups. It is not certain, however, whether the isolated menhirs can be related to the grouped stones, which often consist of simple blocks.

In general, these are rough or roughly-shaped blocks, whose height is greater than their width—though there are some exceptions. Their shape varies considerably, according to the type of rock of which they are made. When a natural block, isolated by erosion, was available, it was used just as it was. A rock which projected even a little could be detached by a still traditional method, which makes use of fire and cold water to split its seams.[1] A menhir of this type has a fresh break on one face and eroded surfaces on the others. This explains the appearance of so many granite menhirs—rounded except on one side. Again, the existence of joints, of fractures with a flat or curved surface, the varying speeds at which rocks deteriorate (especially coarse-grained rocks, which sometimes crumble in a few hundred years in places where the stone is already un-sound), the effect of rain and of water streaming down the surfaces—all these factors explain the curious shapes of many stones; we need not attribute them to the express intentions of the constructors, except in very clear cases, and in connexion with the more durable rocks. Moreover, the menhirs of schist or quartzite always retain their jagged outlines.

THE
MENHIRS

Plate 43

There are, however, several menhirs in Brittany whose shape is so regular that they have obviously been worked. Their surface has been levelled all round by hammering, or rather by shaping with the help of stone mauls. This surface finishing does not, of course, result in a fine polish, but it has nevertheless preserved these large blocks of granite (which were, incidentally, skilfully chosen) from any discernible crumbling. Perhaps the menhir of Champ-Dolent, near Dol (Ille-et-Vilaine), $9\frac{1}{2}$ m. high, could be included in this series. But these shaped menhirs are a peculiarity of western Léon (Finistère); one may mention that of Saint-Gonvarc'h, Landunvez (6 m. high); of Kerenneur or Kerhouézel, Porspoder (over $6\frac{1}{2}$ m.); the standing menhir ($10\frac{1}{2}$ m.) and the inclined menhir ($9\frac{1}{2}$ m.) at Kergadiou, Plourin-Ploudalmeazeau, the former having the most perfect shape of all the menhirs and the latter being unfinished. The menhir of Kerloas (or Kervéatous), Plouarzel,

Plate 42

12 m. high, is the largest still standing; near its base, two bosses in relief, diametrically opposite one another, may be the remains of a more complex piece of sculpture, and were until comparatively recently the object of fertility rites among the peasants, intended to ensure that in the case of newly-married couples the man would sire children and the woman be head of the family.

The general dimensions of the menhirs vary considerably, ranging from less than a metre to more than 20. The giant menhir of Locmariaquer (Morbihan), the Men-er-Hroeg (the 'fairy's stone'), broken into four or five pieces before 1727 (when it was drawn by President de Robien), must have been over 20 m. high, 134 cubic m. in volume, and over 350 metric tons in weight. It may be that it was neither struck by lightning nor shattered by an earth tremor, but was broken while being erected, owing to its having been top-heavy. The menhir of Ile-Melon, Porspoder (Finistère), destroyed during the second World War, was only 7 m. high, but weighed over 80 tons. The largest menhirs still standing are not so heavy, and range

from 9 to 12 m. in height. Those of 7 to 8 m. are fairly numer‑
ous; 25 exceeding 7 m. in height have been counted in Brittany.
A list of the giants with their exact order of precedence would
be deceptive at the moment, since the published heights are
often very inaccurate.

As a rule, a rock was used which was already on the site or
very near it, so that it had to be transported only a short distance
—though in any case the removal was a *tour de force.* Near the
menhir of Men‑Marz at Pontusval, Brignogan (Finistère), can
be seen the rocks from which it was detached. In a number of
instances transportation up to nearly 3 km. can be geologically
demonstrated (such as the menhir of Derlez, Peumerit, Finis‑
tère). These operations were certainly carried out with rollers,
and a route was chosen with as few slopes as possible. A pit
was dug in advance, into which the block had to be tipped,
after being rolled, if necessary, on to a raised embankment,
made of wood or earth and destroyed after the menhir had
finally been wedged in place. In the case of the large stones, the
tipping into position obviously had to be controlled and
guided, and to achieve this, a braking and lubricating sub‑
stance such as fine gravel or grain, slowly sifting from a
wooden chute, may have been used.[2] Once it was upright in
its trench, and firmly wedged with tightly packed stones heaped
round it, the monolith was solidly in place. More rarely, one
finds monoliths with a flat base, simply balanced on end. It is
quite possible that there were also wooden menhirs where no
rock was available.

Excavations at the foot of the menhirs (which are incident‑
ally often dangerous for the monument since they destroy its
packing) have constantly shown that before the erection there
was a ritual burial of objects or a ceremony in the trench.[3]
Remains of charred wood are always found, and stones
reddened by fire. Fairly often, one comes across more definite
archaeological finds—remains of pottery, flakes or implements

Plate 44

of flint, polished axes, grindstones and pestles, pebble tools, strikers, hand polishers, or spindle whorls. Sometimes the pottery includes an almost undamaged pot (Kerlay, Ploban-nalec, and Prat-Palud, Plomeur, Finistère). In some instances, as at the Picaigne, near Saint-Servais (Côtes-du-Nord), the packing round the base covered a small chamber containing charred wood.

The standing stones were inevitably used as landmarks at all periods, and bronze or gold hoards are often found buried in their immediate vicinity, secondarily and adventitiously, as well as debris from the Iron Age and the Gallo-Roman period or even later; one must not be misled by these additions.

It is only very rarely that one finds any engraved or carved decoration on the menhirs. To be more exact, any decoration they may have had was too exposed to weathering to survive (whereas that in the megalithic tombs has long remained hidden deep in the earth). A few instances are known, however: five serpents at Manio, Carnac (Morbihan), axes with handles in relief at Saint-Denec, Porspoder (Finistère) and at Kermarquer, Moustoirac (Morbihan).[4] More frequently, one finds cup-marks, isolated or in groups; these also occur on blocks of stone at all periods—but are often due to natural causes.

It is important not to confuse these megaliths with the clearly geometrically shaped stelae common to the whole of western Brittany, which will be discussed in the section on the Iron Age. Some writers have tried to establish a continuity between the two series of monuments, and in order to do so have arbitrarily attributed to various Bronze Age periods some small fairly well-cut monuments which cannot in fact be thus dated with any degree of certainty.

Single menhirs were probably less frequent than the present scene suggests; isolated stones are often the sole survivors of what was formerly a group; they are found, in any case, more often on the slopes of a hill than on its summit. Some occur in valleys, and in addition a whole series is situated beside water or in a stream.

With the very limited evidence at his disposal, the interpretation of the single menhirs is one of the archaeologist's nightmares, and has given rise to far too much speculative literature. Were they graves? This is far from certain; even when soil conditions are favourable to the preservation of bones, no human bones have been found. Were they boundary posts, commemorative stones, landmarks, idols or fetishes, elements of a phallic cult? The shape of many of them lends some support to the last suggestion, as does a comparison with various standing stones in Africa and Asia. Numerous interesting folk-lore legends exist, which have been analysed by researchers;[5] but all they do is to confirm, if we can accept their evidence, the ritual or 'religious' character of these monuments.

Some menhirs form a special category—those known as 'peritaphic' or 'indicators' (i.e., markers, indicating the position of graves). They are found on or near mounds or barrows, near megalithic tombs, but also at some distance from them. Sometimes the association is obvious; more often it is uncertain and no doubt fortuitous.

The menhirs grouped in twos and threes, which do not form part of an alignment or a definite geometrical structure (for example, a large menhir with a small one a few metres away), present an insoluble problem. These groups are often found in the bottom of valleys (e.g., Pergat, Louargat, Côtes-du-Nord: a giant menhir 10 m. high, and a small one just over 2 m. high, 20 m. away), where perhaps it was desired to mark each important egress with a standing stone.

The complex groupings of menhirs form two large categories: the alignments and the enclosures. They are sometimes found in association. The blocks of stone in these grouped monuments are smaller than the single menhirs, and have usually been left more or less unshaped. The groups may have been rounded off with earthworks and embankments, which being more vulnerable, have usually disappeared.[6] As a general rule, all these groups have been damaged, and from the remains still existing, it is very difficult to form an exact idea of their original appearance. Moreover, a reconstruction based on step-by-step reasoning, from a comparison with similar remains that are perhaps more complete in other respects, is a particularly delicate operation.

THE MEGA-
LITHIC
ENCLO-
SURES

The isolated megalithic enclosures—if, indeed, any of them are really isolated—are basically quadrilaterals, circles or semi-circles. One must be careful not to mistake the kerbstones of a long mound or of a lost megalith for a quadrilateral enclosure. The quadrilateral of Crucuno, Erdeven (Morbihan)—unfortunately we do not know what it was like before its restoration—is a rectangle with an exact east-west orientation; its dimensions are such that the diagonals lie in the direction of the rising sun at the solstices. At Lanvéoc, in the Crozon peninsula (Finistère), there was a square enclosure. On the island of Ouessant (Finistère) there seems to have been a rectangular enclosure divided down the centre by a line of menhirs.

A few groups of small blocks and embankments which have more or less crumbled away, and are therefore particularly fantastic in shape, seem originally to have been part of large and ancient monuments. Also in the Crozon peninsula, the monument of Ty-ar-Huré, near Morgat, in addition to various extensions, still preserves a roughly rectangular central core; this is characterised by a double line of large and small blocks regularly paired together, stepping down towards the interior.

The semicircle of Kergonan, Ile-aux-Moines, in the gulf of Morbihan, seems to be an isolated monument, very symmetrical and regular in shape. There are still 36 menhirs, about 2 to 3 m. high, marking out a half-circle nearly 90 m. in diameter, which must have been completed by stones touching one another throughout the half-circle and across its diameter. The main axis is set at 126°, in the direction of sunrise at the winter solstice.[7] A straight line linking the centre of this monument with the centre of the Er-Lannic group would lie in the direction of the rising sun at the summer solstice.

The latter monument, on the islet of that name—also in the gulf of Morbihan, near its entrance (*commune* of Arzon)—consists of two incomplete circles touching one another, now forming a horseshoe shape.[8] Part of one of them is on dry land; all the rest now lies in the sea, and is only visible at very low tides, owing to the rise in the sea-level that took place in post-Pleistocene times. Some restoration has been carried out, and 49 menhirs from 1 m. to 5 m. 35 high have been re-erected; but some stones that would have been a danger to shipping have been left as they were. The north-south axis of the two circles is 100 m. long; at the point where they touch, there is a large broken menhir originally over 7 m. long. The exact plan of the monument is uncertain, and the restoration has aroused some controversy. It is claimed that the two circles were much more regular, and that the one now beneath the sea has been disturbed by the violence of the currents and the undermining of the substratum. At all events, the menhirs were embedded in a supporting embankment of stones and earth, and surrounded at their base with a well-constructed packing. On each side of the embankment—inside and outside the circle, therefore—there was a series of ritual hearths, protected by small stone constructions. These had been reddened by a fierce fire, and there was a considerable quantity of charred wood. One must remember that the whole island shows traces of intensive occupation, even found in the earth inside the sacred enclosures; this occupation may in part have been of earlier date.

Er-Lannic is the only certain example of a stone-circle on the continent, and differs appreciably from the numerous British monuments of this type.

Groups of several menhirs arranged in a line or lines are unusually plentiful in Brittany. One tends, however, to think of the alignments only in the form of the great parallel rows of Carnac (Morbihan), pictures of which are known throughout the world. Moreover, it is a great pity that these alignments, which enjoyed legal protection at a fairly early date, have also been subject to misdirected restorations—particularly in the nineteenth century—so that it is now nearly impossible to know whether there are in fact any menhirs still in their original place, and one cannot rely on them for the establishment of serious topographical data.[9]

The large groups of alignments, formed of several parallel rows of menhirs or blocks diminishing in size in a definite direction, are most usually found in the areas where there are great concentrations of Passage Graves, though they are also represented elsewhere. In the complete examples, the lines run at right angles to the chord of a semicircle of closely packed menhirs, out of relation to the central axis of the group.

One of the main series of these alignments forms a kind of intermittent barrier between the Etel and Crach rivers (Morbi⁄han);[10] but in fact each group lies in a slightly different direction from the preceding one and is separate from it. At Carnac itself, over a distance of 4 km., there are thus nearly three thousand menhirs still standing. Towards the west, at Ménec, there remain 1169 standing stones, 70 of them forming a semicircle in a mid⁄lateral position, and 1099 in eleven lines averaging 100 m. wide and 1167 m. long. The highest stone is nearly 4 m. tall. The spaces between the lines are clearly marked and are about equal in width. This group seems to end at the very much damaged remains of another semicircle, meeting its curved side formed of contiguous stones. After a gap of over 240 m., at Kermario, 1029 menhirs are grouped in ten lines (average width 100 m., length 1120 m.); nothing survives of the semi⁄circle which was the starting point of this alignment, except for

Plates 46, 47

Plate 48

its completely cleared site. The largest menhir (still overturned) is 6 m. high. This group, continuing up hill and down dale, crossing the course of a stream in which menhirs could still be seen in their place not so long ago (before the construction of a dam), presents some local anomalies; notably, near the farm of Kermario, three transversal contiguous menhirs on its southern side—no doubt the remains of an earlier monument. Near Manio, the alignment passes over an unchambered long mound, with its menhir lying in the opposite direction— there is thus here a stratigraphy by superposed construction. In the same way, the Passage Grave situated at the corner of the presumed site of the semicircle must have been earlier than the alignments, but has since lost its barrow. At the eastern end of this group, a little beyond Manio, one can guess where it ends close against some remains of the arc of a semicircle, because of the embankments, which seem to correspond with a structure visible in aerial photographs. After another gap of 393 m., the Kerlescan group with 598 stones in all, begins to the west, with a semicircle of which 43 stones remain; the packing of 30 others has also been found. The northern side of this enclosure passes above a long mound in the upper layers of which have been found a pot deriving from the Beaker type and a flat copper axe. The rows of menhirs, with 555 stones in 13 lines, over a width of 139 m. at the starting point, with a gap of 200 m. behind the village, end with a few lines in a different direction. The tallest standing stone is nearly 4 m. high.

Many of these menhirs stand on the actual rock, or nearly so. At Kermario, excavations at their base have produced remains similar to those found at the foot of the isolated menhirs: flints, including an arrow-head, fragments of pottery, pebble tools (one striker), a polished axe, a quern, stones reddened by fire, and, most frequently, cinders and ash.

In the same region, at rather greater intervals towards the west, one finds again at Vieux-Moulin, Plouharnel, 6 blocks belonging to a semicircle, and at Sainte-Barbe 50 menhirs, nearly all overthrown; finally near Erdeven, at Kerzerho, there are 1129 menhirs in 10 lines, extending for 2105 m.; the total width is 64 m., and there are numerous uncertain extensions in the woods. A line of 23 menhirs and 6 fragments lies at right angles to the series, which includes two stones more than 6 m. high and a menhir with cupmarks.

Elsewhere, at Saint-Pierre-Quiberon, near Le-Moulin, there are 24 menhirs in 5 lines; farther on are the remains of a semi-circle with 25 menhirs. At Locmariaquer there seems to have been a monument whose form can no longer be determined.

Outside the Morbihan district, too, we find groups of men-hirs. Between Penmarch and Plomeur (Finistère), the align-ments of La-Madeleine and Lestrigniou consisted of nearly 500 stones at the beginning of last century; towards the end of it there were still 200, in 4 lines stretching for about 1 km. Now, only a few stones remain, and most of these are over-turned. In the Crozon peninsula (Finistère), at Lostmarc'h, there are 11 stones, marking the remains of three parallel lines.

At Pleslin (Côtes-du-Nord), there remains a good group of 65 menhirs, in 5 lines, the last representatives of a much larger ensemble. At Langon, the 'Demoiselles' comprise 37 stones in 6 lines. At Arbourg, near Herbignac (Loire-Atlantique), there were still 57 stones in 7 lines in the last century.

But in addition to these large groups of menhirs, there exist various categories of simpler alignments—simpler in appear-ance, at least. Of course, any two standing stones form a 'line'; but there must be at least three in a row before one can presume that the alignment is intentional. In all the certain instances of this kind that are fairly well preserved, one finds that the menhirs are only a few metres apart, as in the larger assemblages of alignments.

A remarkable series of small alignments once covered the Crozon peninsula (Finistère),[11] but they have greatly deteriorated during the last few decades. At Leuré there were two lines at right angles to one another, while at Landaoudec a very complicated group contained, until about the middle of last century, nearly 300 menhirs, extending for 400 m., with numerous transversal rows. At Lostmarc'h there are a few remains of three parallel lines, and at Raguénès of two rows at right angles. At the present time, the most spectacular ensemble is that of Lagatjar, Camaret (restored a few decades ago), with a main axis more than 200 m. long, two lines running from it at right angles and another obliquely; it must originally have extended still further.

Plate 49

Lines of menhirs are often found in the central hilly regions of Brittany: at Saint-Goazec, Spézet (Finistère), and Roudou-allec (Morbihan) in the Montagnes Noires, in the forests of Haute-Sève and Fougères, on the heathlands of Saint-Just (Ille-et-Vilaine). A more complicated group is that on the moorlands of Saint-Michel, Brasparts (Finistère).

At the foot of the menhirs in these latter alignments, one still finds the same kind of remains as at the bottom of the sockets of the isolated menhirs (e.g. the three menhirs of Kerfland, Plomeur, Finistère); some have served as landmarks for later hoards (Middle Bronze Age hoard at Penhoat, Coray, Finistère).

Whether the groups are large or small, it is obviously extremely difficult to interpret these monuments. It merely begs the question to say that these constructions were of religious or ritual character; this applies just as much to the isolated menhirs. From the fact that some of the lines (which, to tell the truth, are not always perfectly straight) seem to be orientated in a systematic fashion, attempts have been made to build up systems of astronomical (or even astrological) magic or religion, of considerable complexity. In this speculative domain of megalithic orientations, the subject has been confused and discredited by the works of various writers with somewhat fanciful ideas.[12] This is all the more regrettable since there are certain unquestionable facts; but even the best workers on the subject have themselves tended to go a little too far in their interpretations, out of a desire to systematise their findings. The most reasonable theory, carried to its conclusion, finds lines of menhirs approximating to all the following orientations, corresponding with the direction of the sunrise at the indicated dates (and inversely, of the sunset):

EQUINOXES (March 21, September 21) 90°
    Meridian, perpendicular to the equinoxial sunrises 0°

SOLSTICES:
    Summer (June 21) 54°
    Winter (December 21) 126°
    Perpendicular to the solsticial sunrises 144°

INTERMEDIARY SUNRISES (corresponding to dates half-way between the solstices and the equinoxes):
    Intermediary summer sunrises (May 6, August 8) 66°
    Intermediary winter sunrises (November 8, February 4) 114°
    Perpendicular to the intermediary sunrises $\begin{cases} 156° \\ 24° \end{cases}$

(The angles given are those valid in general for the average latitude of Brittany; for some, one should take into account geographical or temporal variations.)

In fact, the correspondence between the orientation of the monuments, as far as this can be determined (for nothing is more indefinite than the principal point of a menhir), and the theoretical orientations is fairly elastic. It must be admitted that in some cases it is astonishing, and in others it has no very clear significance, especially since the elements of any single line of menhirs are often scarcely in alignment. Of course, one would have to take into account the height of the curtain of trees on the horizon at the time when they were erected. But in any case it can be seen that the possible orientations as listed in the above table are so numerous that, with a margin of error of several degrees to either side of the theoretical value, the sectors corres' ponding to a large number of neighbouring orientations partly overlap. In other words, confronted with any line of menhirs, one could easily make it correspond with some supposedly intentional orientation.

However, there is no doubt that many of the rows of menhirs are 'orientated'; but perhaps not always for astronomical reasons. Therefore, extreme caution is necessary here; likewise in attempting to find orientation, on the geodesic scale, as it were, between groups of monuments often at a considerable distance from each other, and especially the large menhirs.[13] In some instances, one can say that there may have been an in' tentional marking'out; in many others, one cannot in all honesty make such a claim.

All this does not shed any very clear light on the function of the menhirs; whether isolated or in groups, they remain en' shrouded in mystery. This is no doubt why their study has, unjustifiably, been comparatively neglected.

CHAPTER VIII

The Armorican Barrow Culture

METAL MADE its first appearance with the Chalco-lithic complex, but this culture can only be considered as a preliminary phase whose various elements were super-imposed on local cultural groups of a pure Neolithic tradition. The first true metal civilisation in western Armorica, on the other hand, is represented in a group of barrows; it forms a homogeneous whole, possesses its own monuments, and reveals an abrupt change in funerary customs: single-grave individual inhumation in a closed chamber beneath a barrow replaces the collective graves of traditional Neolithic type. Even where stone is used, the products are definitely original, both in shape and finish. Moreover, new metallurgical types appear: triangular daggers, flat-bladed swords, halberds, axes with slight rims, and pins. Finally, some general characteristics link this group with the cultures of the classic centres of the European Early Bronze Age ('Unĕtice, El Argar), or the most archaic elements of the barrow culture of Germany and eastern France (Forest of Haguenau). But the closest relationship, observed at the very beginning of comparative archaeological studies, is with the Wessex Culture of southern England.[1]

The Bronze Age barrows were discovered and excavated at an early date in Armorica (Lothéa, Quimperlé, Finistère, 1843; Tanwedou near Bourbriac, Côtes-du-Nord, 1865). They were first thought to be megalithic chambers, but were later identified as belonging to the Bronze Age.

The only evidence we have concerning this culture is pro-vided almost entirely by the graves. Indeed, dwelling sites are extremely rare at all epochs in Armorica; two small villages of 40 to 50 habitations each, at Reuniou near Brennilis (Finistère), have been ascribed to this period, but such dating seems very

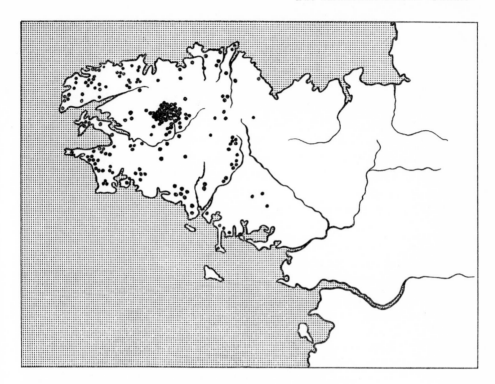

Fig. 31 General distribution map of the Armorican Bronze Age barrows

uncertain. Moreover, hoards are very rare in the Early Bronze
Age, and still infrequent at the beginning of the Middle Bronze
Age; so that metal articles belonging to the barrow culture are
hardly ever found, except secondarily, in more recent hoards.

One has to fall back, therefore, on the architecture and the
grave-goods of the tombs, and the geographical distribution of
the latter.[2] The general distribution of the Bronze Age barrows
is, in fact, strictly localised to the west of a line running from
the Bay of Saint-Brieuc to the mouth of the Vilaine. They are
regularly spaced along the coast, and in the interior there is a

Fig. 31

I

large concentration along the Blavet, and particularly along the southern edge of the Monts d'Arrée. A study of their grave-goods makes it possible to distinguish two successive series.

Their general shape is that of a somewhat flattened spherical dome. Actually, many have been ploughed out in the course of cultivating the ground, or exploited for making threshing floors or sowing beds. Often, when the barrow is levelled, a capstone or slab covering the chamber is revealed—looking like a

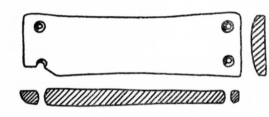

Fig. 32 Wrist-guard of polished schist, with four holes, from the barrow at Lothéa, Forest of Carnoët, Quimperlé (F.). ⅔

natural rock flush with the surface of the ground—or catches in the blade of the plough. These barrows have an average diameter of 20 to 30 m., the largest being 50 m. across. The disturbance of the ground by cultivation often renders their outline somewhat uncertain. The best-preserved specimens are as much as 5 to 6 m. above the ground (Tanwedou, Bour-briac).

The bulk of the barrow is usually composed of earth or clay, and there is sometimes a small cairn protecting the central chamber. More rarely, the whole of the barrow consists of stones (Kervini, Poullan, Finistère).

The chamber may be built in various ways. In some barrows of the Trégor district (which also have a certain number of archaic characteristics), there are traces of wooden structures. Not only was the occupant buried in a cavity roofed with wooden beams, but the grave-goods were enclosed in small wooden boxes.

However, this first series also contains tombs with large slabs, no doubt under the influence of megalithic techniques. One or two slabs are used in addition to the covering one, and in southern Finistère there are even some tombs that are entirely megalithic (Kerlivit, Pouldergat; Kerhué-Bras, Plonéour-Lanvern; Lothéa, Quimperlé).

Not more than one tomb per barrow has ever been found in this series, and one notes the following division of architectural styles: 7 tombs with wooden structures; 1 tomb with dry stone corbelling; 8 tombs with megalithic structures or cists; 3 tombs with a simple covering slab; 12 tombs with a slab resting on walls of dry stone construction.

The distinction between the two successive series of barrows is based on a study of their grave-goods. The basic characteristics of the first series are the persistence of stone material, the abundance of metal articles, and the absence of pottery in the chamber.

Large, long objects made of polished stone have sometimes been found, and described as 'sceptres' or 'whetstones'. Some which are flattened and perforated seem to have been better fitted for the latter use. Archers' wrist-guards of schist are fairly rare (Coatjou-Glas, Plonéis; Lothéa, Quimperlé—the latter having four holes).

The most remarkable objects, however, are the tanged and barbed arrow-heads. These have often been called 'Armorican', though like the barrows they are almost exclusively confined to Lower Brittany. These arrow-heads are usually of fine honey-coloured or grey flint, sometimes of translucent quartz. The number found in a tomb varies from two or three items to several dozen—up to about fifty (forty-six at Tossen-Rugouec, Prat, Côtes-du-Nord). Their arrangement in the tomb varies; they may be in small wooden boxes, among stones, lying loose, or set out as at Kerguévarec, Plouyé (Finistère), where

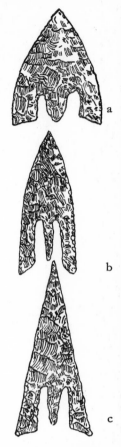

Fig. 33 Types of Armorican arrow-heads: a, short ogival type (barrow of Kerhué-Bras, Plonéour-Lanvern, F.); b, long ogival type (barrow of Tossen-Maharit, Trévérec, C.-du-N.); c, triangular (barrow of Cruguel, Guidel, M.). All ½

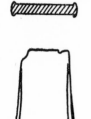

Fig. 34 Axe with slight flanges from the barrow of Tossen-Maharit, Trévérec (C.-du-N.). ½

Plate 50

they were laid in a circle round a jet spacing-bead of the same type as were used for the crescent-shaped necklaces. These arrows are very fine—about 1 mm. or so thick—and of an extremely harmonious ogival or triangular shape. They are works of art or luxury articles destined for a funerary rôle, and are only found in graves. A few, however, were mounted on a wooden shaft about 10 cm. long.

Metal is fairly plentiful in this culture. The axes usually have a slight flange, and are up to 20 cm. long. These, too, are sometimes ceremonial weapons, especially those where the blade is decorated with parallel lines. In one case a median line forms the beginning of a heel. Some specimens still bear traces of a wooden haft.

With the exception of a few small tanged daggers, or the curious dagger with an undulating blade from Kerhué-Bras, Plonéour-Lanvern (Finistère), the weapons have a flat, triangular blade. The 'Armorican' or Breton type is characterised by a little half-moon opening in the hilt-plate below the guard, and especially by a short tang or tongue penetrating the hilt. This is of wood, or very occasionally of metal, and fixed to the blade with four or six pins or rivets. The hilt is decorated with thousands of tiny gold nails, geometrically arranged in rows of chevrons. Fragments of leather sheaths are decorated in the same way.

The 'swords' are really a slightly longer form of dagger. The half-moon opening below the guard, and the little tongue, are also found in them; both swords and daggers sometimes have their blades decorated with fine lines engraved parallel to the cutting edge. The halberds or 'dagger-axes' can be identified either by the way their blade thickens in the centre or by their asymmetrical guard—two rivets on one side and three on the other (Bel-Air, Landerneau, Finistère).

Among the other metal articles, arrow-heads are very rare (Saint-Fiacre, Melrand, Morbihan); more important are the ring-headed dress pins found in two barrows of the Trégor, very close to the Unětice type and thus appearing as evidence of links with central Europe.

The poor state of preservation of some articles makes identification impossible. A very large proportion of the metal objects in these barrows is much damaged through electrolysis in the soil. From the metallurgical point of view, one still finds a few articles of arsenical copper;[3] most objects already contain an appreciable proportion of tin, as well as retaining some arsenic, bronze weapons without arsenic being still infrequent.

There is no pottery amongst the grave-goods in the first series of barrows. Nevertheless, one occasionally finds fragments of Late Neolithic type in the mass of heaped-up earth.

The geographical distribution of these barrows shows greater density in the coastal regions. The oldest group is perhaps that of the Trégor, with its chambers roofed with wood, and its pins of the Unětice type. Diffusion took place in the direction of Finistère, where there are two zones of concentration—in the north-east, and in the south-west. In the other regions of Lower Brittany the density is less; but it is interesting to observe occasional examples in the interior, these having penetrated up the river valleys (Aulne, Blavet).

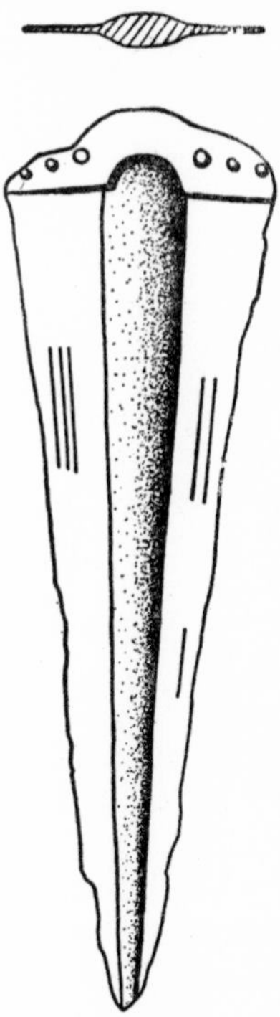

Just 30 barrows in all can be attributed to this series, in which the furniture is very homogeneous (27 have between them produced the beautiful arrow-heads); and it probably represents a fairly short period of time.

Fig. 35 Dagger from the barrow of Cruguel, Guidel (M.); blade with mid-rib. ⅓

The outward appearance of the monument remains the same, possibly with the squatter form predominating. One also occasionally finds several tombs protected by a single mound, as at Kervingar, Plouarzel (Finistère).[4] In this example, it has been shown by the structures, that two small tombs had been built first, each with its own barrow; then the central chamber

THE
BARROWS
OF THE
SECOND
SERIES

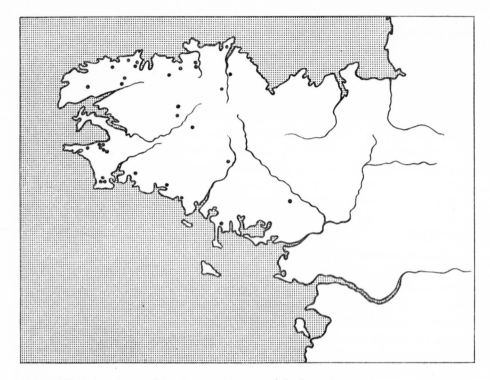

Fig. 36 Distribution map of the Armorican barrows of the first series

was dug (near each cavity flattened heaps of subsoil have been found, resulting from this digging); eventually the final barrow covered the whole group.

The funerary chamber is usually a rectangular cavity lined with dry stone walls, with a large capstone as cover. Two small lateral ledges, of stone, sand or wood, supported an oak flooring which raised the grave-goods from the ground. In addition, it is not unusual to find a false ceiling, also of wood, at half the height of the walls. The dry stone walls are sometimes of almost mathematical regularity.

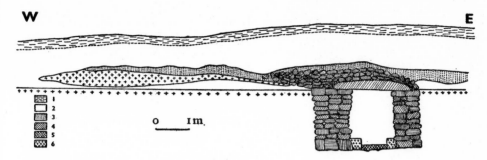

Fig. 37 *Section of the barrow at Kervingar, Plouarzel (F.): 1, humus; 2, at the upper level, earth re-covering the three tombs; at the lower level, ancient soil; 3, layer of grey clay covering the three tombs; 4, stones and slabs; 5, decayed wood; 6, weathered granitic rubble, from the sub-soil, utilized for the ledges, and also found in a heap coming from the digging out of the principal burial vault. The section only cuts the principal chamber*

There are two other types of construction, in addition to the dry stone vaults. The use of wooden cists, although it is going out, has not disappeared. In this case the monument may include a horseshoe-shaped enclosure, from the middle of which, towards the interior, runs a little pebbly spur covering the cist (Keranbroc'h, Rosporden, Finistère). Some tombs are built with corbelling, particularly in regions where schistose rocks are available; there are also several cases with walls which

Fig. 38

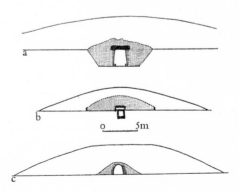

Fig. 38 *Sections of the barrows of: a, Penker, Plabennec (F.). Chamber with dry stone walls, capstone, and ledges supporting a wood flooring; b, Kervastal, Plonéis (F.). Chamber entirely built of jointed slabs, with double ceiling; c, section of a barrow at Coatmocun, Brennilis (F.). Corbelled chamber of dry stones*

converge slightly towards the top and which are roofed with a large slab. Megalithic techniques are therefore still used, and even perfected. In addition to the fine examples of massive stone-built chambers, there are smaller ones that are really carefully-built little cists. The blocks used, especially those of schistose nature, have been worked and shaped so as to fit together. In the barrow of Kervastal, Plonéis (Finistère), in addition to these improvements there was a floor consisting of a large flat stone, and a double ceiling of two superimposed covering stones.

Any statistics concerning the tomb type are bound to be somewhat invalidated by the existence of tombs without grave-goods, or, conversely, of tombs whose grave-goods we possess, but whose architectural characteristics were not recorded by the finder. Of the tombs where both goods and structure are known, there are about: 4 with wooden construction; 8 with dry stone corbelling; 15 with megalithic structures or cists; 35 with a capstone resting on dry stone walls.

The grave-goods from the second series of barrows are characterised chiefly by the disappearance of the stone elements, the rarity of metal articles, and the abundance of pottery.

Stone objects are almost entirely absent. There remain nothing but flint flakes, fragments of quartz and pieces of shale—ubiquitous material that could be the result of infiltration. The only exception is the Mané-Coh-Clour site, Carnac (Morbihan), where a four-handled pot was accompanied by a tanged and barbed arrow-head (of a Neolithic type) and a polished axe of dolerite. Possibly this may be an instance of the re-utilisation of a tomb—unless these were objects that had been picked up and used as talismans.

Metal weapons become less frequent. The types remain the same for axes (which are very rare) and daggers, henceforth the most commonly found bronze objects, swords and halberds apparently having disappeared. At Kersaint-Plabennec (Finis-

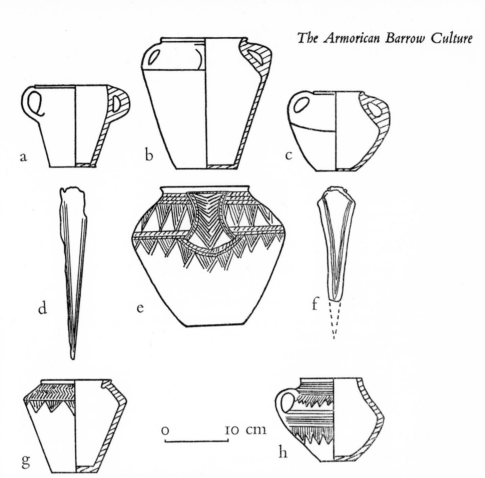

Fig. 39 Types of pots and daggers from the second series of Armorican barrows: a, b, c, barrow with three chambers of Kervingar, Plouarzel (F.); d, barrow of Coatalio, Fouesnant (F.); e, barrow of Ruguello, Trézény (C.-du-N.); f, barrow of Kersaint-Plabennec (F.); g, barrow of Parc-Vouden, Guidel (M.); h, barrow of Kergoz, Plounevez-Loc'hrist (F.)

tère) a slightly more developed dagger was found: the edge of the blade becomes concave, widening at the base, and the engraved lines that decorate it meet before reaching the point. The dagger of Kervellerin, Cléguer (Morbihan) is also of an

Plate 51

evolved type. Generally, only one dagger in association with one pot is found in the graves of this series. Finally, the decoration of the hilts with little gold nails has almost disappeared, since only a single instance has been found (La-Garenne, Saint-Jean-Brévelay, Morbihan).

Fig. 39

Pottery, on the other hand, is plentiful, although there is usually only one unbroken pot in each tomb. The known specimens—of which there are about 80, including the broken ones—vary in size and type. The ware is fairly coarse, with gritty *degraissant*; its general appearance is crude and the profiles often asymmetrical (possibly accentuated by deformation during firing).

Plate 52

The classic type, known as 'Armorican', is a biconical urn with four handles, arranged diametrically opposite one another, two and two. Types with fewer handles, or with none, are fairly frequent, while the enormous six-handled pot from Launay-Boloi, Pleumeur-Gauthier (Côtes-du-Nord), remains unique. Out of the 80, three are indeterminate, nine without handles, 14 with one handle, nine with two handles, four with three handles, 40 with four handles and 1 with six. These ribbon-shaped handles are very wide; usually one end is attached to the rim of the pot and the other at the junction of the two cones forming the body of the vessel.

Plates 53–59

The four-handled pots seldom have any decoration, though this is found more frequently on the other forms. The geometrical patterns are made up of alternating parallel lines, chevrons, oblique strokes and hatched triangles. The decorated area is often confined to the upper cone, the lower part simply having a single row of motifs round the base. The handles are included in the decoration. The motifs are those found in the great European Bronze Age centres. Some rather clumsy pots of thick ware are slightly reminiscent of Late Neolithic forms.

Fig. 40

The geographical distribution of barrows of the second series reveals, in the north of Brittany, a shifting towards western Léon, the Trégor being abandoned. They became more numerous in

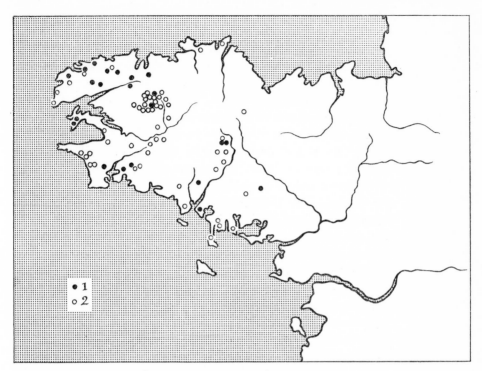

Fig. 40 Distribution map of the Armorican barrows of the second series: 1, with pot and dagger; 2, with pot alone

other zones, but the large concentrations of the Monts d'Arrée and of the upper valley of the Blavet are particularly note‐worthy.

Early archaeologists considered that it was of the utmost importance to know whether the funerary rite was by inhuma‐tion or incineration. In fact, for various reasons very few remains of bones have been found. Usually the bone has com‐pletely disintegrated—or only a few fragments survive, some‐times fossilised by the salts from metal objects; teeth are among

THE
FUNERARY
RITES OF
THE
BARROW
CULTURE

the traces which best resist decay. In a few cases, however, skeletons or parts of skeletons have been found in good condition. A considerable amount of organic debris, especially decomposed wood, has been classified as 'human ashes', without containing the least trace of burnt bones, or even of charred wood. Where there is a rectangular vault (1 m. by 2 m. on an average) which is large enough for a corpse, inhumation seems probable. In the case of small tombs, in cists or in corbelled dry-walled chambers, and where wood cinders or fragments of burnt bones have indeed been found, we may reasonably assume that incineration took place.

Considerable precautions were taken to ensure the comfort and preservation of the dead man's remains. We may recall briefly the protective impermeable covering of clay, or arrangements such as stones fitting closely together to seal the chamber hermetically, and the overhang of the capstone, to prevent infiltration. Wooden ledges raise the floor off the bottom of the chamber, which is sometimes arranged like a sump; occasionally there is also a false ceiling at half the height of the chamber. The bottom of the chamber is often covered with fine sand— river sand or sea sand according to the locality. The head of the corpse may rest on a little clay cushion. At Berrien (Finistère), where one of the barrows contained a skeleton lying on its back, fragments of leather pierced with little holes have been found; the body was probably wrapped in a shroud of skins, sewn up with linen thread. At Kergoniou, Guisseny (Finistère), it was once thought that the skull showed traces of *post-mortem* trepanning and removal of pieces, whereas actually it was a case of the partial dissolution of the skeleton caused by maceration on the part of the corpse's own fermentation liquids.[5]

Weapons are usually placed to the left of the body of the dead (probably right-handed). Pots are also put on the left, but near the head or shoulder, and are sometimes lying on their side. They never contain ashes, and it is a mistake to regard them

as cinerary urns. Among those found, one had been covered
with a linen cloth, of which a few threads still adhered to the
rim. These vessels must have contained food or drink.

Tombs of children may be smaller than those of adults, but
this is not invariably so: the large barrow of Kersaint-Plabennec
covered a chamber 2 m. by 1 m. containing a four-handled
pot, a dagger, and bone remains that could only have belonged   Plate 52
to a child about six years old (milk teeth and the first signs of
permanent teeth, incipient molars). This was probably the only
occupant of the vast barrow.

Particularly in the case of schist, there are sometimes engravings on the stone slabs of these tombs. They are in a different
style from the designs in the true megalithic tombs, and consist
of dotted circles of cupmarks, groups of small cupmarks in a
surround, or unidentified motifs.

Out of 200 to 250 barrows which can with some probability   THE
be attributed to this Armorican Bronze Age culture, only a   BARROWS
little over a hundred have produced grave-goods enabling them   WITHOUT
to be classified in the first or second series. Some were violated,   GRAVE-
either in early times or at a more recent date, and only through   GOODS
their style of architecture can we ascribe them to the Bronze
Age. When they are near barrows which contained typical
material, it is reasonable to suppose that they belong to the same
group, since there is a tendency for these monuments to be
grouped together in series on unfertile plateaux. Such groups of
barrows are often found in the second series; and—at least pro-
visionally—it is more reasonable to attribute to this second series
all the monuments without grave-goods.

There are, however, some barrows where, in spite of adequate
excavation, no internal chamber or definite structure has been
found. Sometimes a little heap of stones, clay or sand has been
revealed—this can be compared with a heap of stones in the
Kervingar barrow, Plouarzel, placed symmetrically in relation

to the two other little peripheral tombs. These dummy monuments were once considered to be imitation graves—cenotaphs raised to the memory of the departed.

Now, without entirely dismissing this interpretation in every case, one must also consider the barrows which have no chamber, but where there is funerary equipment dispersed throughout the mound of earth, or collected together in a definite spot, and sometimes the remains of bones as well. As in the case of the barrows with chambers, but often in a much larger quantity, this scattered material includes both Late Neolithic artifacts (fragments of pottery, flints, axes, pendants) and pieces of vessels similar to those found in Bronze Age chambers. This definitely suggests that the two cultures were contemporaneous.

Accompanying the barrows, one often finds series of small mounds containing little rectangular cists. A few rare instances have produced grave-goods, but most are empty. Perhaps they were intended for people of less wealth or importance.

PROBLEMS CONNECTED WITH THE SERIES OF BARROWS The existence of two series whose contents differ so widely sets us a number of problems. The hypothesis of a differentiation according to sex—tombs of men containing weapons, and those of women, pottery—is untenable, since male skeletons have been found near pots. Moreover, the geographical distribution of the two series reveals marked differences incompatible with this hypothesis.[6] A chronological succession is therefore the most plausible.

The first series possesses additionally a certain number of archaic characteristics, such as the use of flint arrow-heads, and pins of the Unĕtice type from the beginning of the Early Bronze Age, and, generally, artifacts of arsenical copper. In the second series, on the other hand, stone objects have disappeared, and weapons are all of real bronze; motifs of the Middle Bronze Age appear in the decoration of the pottery. The relationship between the two series is very close from the architectural point of view, and somewhat tenuous as regards the grave-goods. Daggers are of more or less the same type, it is true; but there are no transitional cases showing, for example, four-handled pots in association with arrow-heads. There must have been a sudden partial change in funerary rites—unless we are dealing with two different waves of invaders.

The intrusive elements of the Armorican Barrow Culture must have encountered traditional Neolithic groups. Perhaps they even made use of local labour in the construction of the tombs, which would account for the use of techniques belonging to the megalithic tradition. Conversely, some groups of the Neolithic tradition (e.g. the Carnac group) adopted more or less exactly the funerary rites of the Barrow Culture.

It is relatively easy to find a number of links with this culture in most of the Bronze Age centres in Europe. Unětice influences are revealed by the presence of typical pins; the pottery resembles the Adlerberg type, though at the same time one must admit there is a family likeness to all the pottery in use at this period. The very fact that this is a barrow culture indicates strong affinities with the important Barrow Cultures of Central Europe, and attempts have been made to find a possible derivation by way of an overland route, the intermediary stages being the tombs of Singleyrac (Dordogne) and of Saint-Menoux (Allier), or the finds at Cissac (Gironde); but all these links are very vague.

The closest relationships, however, are with the Wessex Culture of England. There one finds the same type of daggers, similarly decorated sometimes with microscopic gold nails, the 'whetstones', and a limited number of comparable flint arrow-heads, which do not, however, constitute a very close parallel. This resemblance has sometimes been taken to indicate a Breton origin for the Wessex Culture, and at other times a

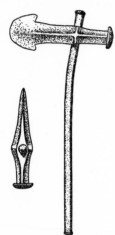

Fig. 41 Hafted battle-axe from Kersoufflet, Le Faouët (M.). $\frac{1}{9}$

Wessex derivation for the Armorican barrows. The hypothesis of a common origin which must be sought in the direction of the northern forms of the Germanic Barrow Culture has been suggested with a greater degree of probability, and the use of a maritime route via the North Sea and the English Channel. Moreover, the Armorican daggers and their Wessex counter- parts have been compared to those of the Oder-Elbe group—a certain number of finds particularly in the Pas-de-Calais and Normandy providing possible stepping-stones. It should be pointed out that these connecting links, whether graves or isolated objects, are very sporadic, and it is difficult to establish a parallel with typical examples of the two series of Armorican barrows. Moreover, even if the various complete dagger blades recorded appear to be of the Breton type, the only surviving arrow-head from the barrows of Beaumont-Hague (Manche) is very unlike the Breton specimens.[7] The presence in the Channel Islands of monuments resembling the internal struc- tures of Armorican barrows, and of biconical pots (the four- handled pot of La-Houge-de-Millais, Jersey, is the most typical), seems more probably the result of a returning tide.

At all events, not only was the English Channel the route by which the Barrow Culture reached Brittany; it also remained throughout its existence a highway affording contact with countries of a related culture. From the anthropological point of view, it should be noted that the skeleton of the Kergoniou barrow, Guissény[5], has been shown to be close to the proto- Nordic types of the so-called 'Corded' race—a fact which con- firms the possibility of a Northern origin for the culture. Such an origin would also explain certain partial affinities acquired in the course of the journey—for example, the introduction of the battle-axe, probably of copper alloy, with a haft also of metal, of Kersoufflet, Le Faouët (Morbihan).

Fig. 41

The trade in certain articles makes it possible to establish links between the historical regions of the Near East and the proto⁄historical cultures of Western Europe which give some idea of the absolute dates. Unfortunately, since these dates can be considered as a *terminus ante quem* as well as *terminus a quo*, they have given rise to two different chronological systems, long and short. The amber plates used as spacing beads are found in Mycenaean shaft graves of about 1525 B.C. or in the tholos of Kakovatos, also in Greece, dating from about 1450, as well as in the early barrows in central Germany. The Armorican barrows of the first series have yielded only one typical amber spacer bead (Saint⁄Fiacre, Melrand), but an imitation of jet has also been found (Kerguévarec, Plouyé) as well as a curious box of gold foil related to the same sort of articles (La Motta, Lannion, Côtes⁄du⁄Nord).

Plate 50

Another source of cross⁄dating is a biconical bead of blue faïence from the tomb of Run⁄ar⁄Justicou, at Kerstrobel, Crozon (Finistère), similar to beads from the tombs of Prosymna, which date from the Late Helladic period (1600⁄1200 B.C.); three specimens have been found in a barrow of North Molton, Devonshire, in association with segmented beads.[8] Now, the barrow of Kerstrobel is of the second Armorican series.

The homogeneity, the limited numbers and the coastal situation of the first series of barrows suggest that this series was relatively of much shorter duration than the second, which evidently lasted for a fairly long period—though probably not beyond the fully developed Middle Bronze Age. The wooden flooring of the central tomb of the Kervingar barrow, Plouarzel, has been dated by the radio⁄carbon method to 1350 ± 50 B.C., a date which fits in well with archaeological forecasts.

K

CHAPTER IX

The Armorican Hoards of the Middle and Late Bronze Age

THE WORD 'HOARD' is used to designate a collection of objects intentionally hidden, usually by burial in the earth. A hoard therefore differs from the goods of a tomb and from material which may be found in a dwelling site, or even from objects found in isolation. Hoards are not confined to the Bronze Age—one finds buried collections of polished stone axes from the Neolithic cultures; but their numbers increased prodigiously during the Bronze Age, and in Armorica they become almost the only material for study from the Middle and Late Bronze Ages.

It is easy to understand the reason for this practice; the first metal objects must have been of great value, and the earth played the part of a strong-box (though the owner did not always come back to recover his property). The custom persisted in all later periods, and at any time of uncertainty hoards of money or jewels were again frequently buried in the ground.

The hoards can be subdivided into several categories according to their contents. 'Merchants' hoards' contain new tools or weapons, often showing traces of the burr from the moulds. Only one or two types are found, repeated in a great number of specimens. They represent the stock-pile of the pedlar who could not afford to risk his entire fortune. This theory of the merchant setting off and being killed on his travels, leaving future generations to discover his precious hoard, has often been criticised; but the fact that another vessel (empty) is often found buried near a hoard may seem to provide evidence in favour of the hypothesis of a shop-storehouse. The 'founder's hoards' contain a varying number of implements, usually broken. Some writers have claimed that the broken swords appear just when iron was beginning to replace bronze; but from the time of the Middle Bronze Age there are fine hoards containing a great many pieces of broken swords. Moreover, as well as damaged weapons intended for melting down, one finds traces of an artisan industry—residues of bronze or copper which on cooling have retained the internal shape of the cruci- ble which had contained them, quantities of mould plugs, metal castings, spoilt articles and the smallest drops of molten metal, show how much importance was attached to the collec- tion of every scrap of the precious material.

The more humble 'domestic hoards' contain only the few tools of a peasant or a small artisan. Sometimes there are some broken weapons, awaiting the next visit of the travelling smith, who would collect them. The 'votive hoards' may represent an offering to the 'nature spirits' or the 'gods'; they can sometimes be identified by a particular arrangement (in a triangle, for example) or by being deposited in a place which, if not dedi- cated to religious ceremonies, was at least a consecrated spot (a river, a lake, a peat-bog, etc.). The 'monetary hoards' may date from the end of the Bronze Age. It should be noted that if a hoard represented a considerable value, the objects in it could be bartered for various commodities. However, when iron began to supplant bronze, some articles were only of use as money, since their composition (an excessive proportion of lead) made them quite useless for any practical purposes. This is the case, notably, with the socketed axes. Of course, all these different types are found with variations, and one is often un- certain in which category a hoard should be placed, especially when the condition in which it was found is not definitely known. There are even cases where there may be confusion with grave-goods. It is not impossible that many of these hoards were buried near inhabited sites, in which case pieces of pottery or flint may be found near-by.

Because of the inaccuracy of descriptions of early discoveries, or even their absence, the estimated numbers of the hoards should perhaps be accepted with caution. The number known, moreover, is well below the possible total. Generally, in fact, we only have records of such as have been discovered comparatively recently; those which came to light earlier were only noticed if there was anything remarkable about their size or their contents. The number of hoards known in Brittany can be estimated as 388, distributed as follows:[1]

Finistère:	146
Côtes-du-Nord:	102
Morbihan:	65
Ille-et-Vilaine:	39
Loire-Atlantique:	36

The number of articles in a hoard varies considerably. It may only contain one or two items, but in this case it must be distinguished from isolated objects by characteristics which show that the burial was intentional: it may be in a pot, beneath a stone, or in a carefully constructed cavity. In the case of 'monetary hoards' principally consisting of socketed axes, the old accounts give staggering figures; one sometimes finds reference to a horse-load, or to thousands of implements (4,000 at Maure-de-Bretagne, Ille-et-Vilaine). These figures are often exaggerated, but in some authentic cases the number may well have reached 1,000. In 1959 a hoard of 800 socketed axes was found at Saint-Bugan, Loudéac (Côtes-du-Nord), and another of 900 at Guesman, Le-Tréhou (Finistère). The total weight of a hoard varies according to its components; and in some cases it is considerably augmented by ingots which may weigh from 3 to 4 kg. (7 to 8 lb.), but in an average hoard the weight varies between 10 and 50 kg. (20 to 100 lb.).

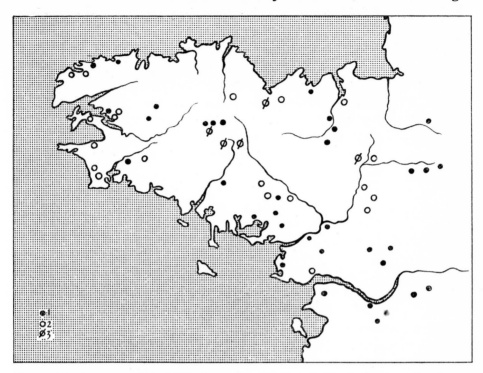

Fig. 42 Distribution map of the Middle Bronze Age hoards: 1, hoards of palstaves; 2, hoards of the Tréboul type; 3, hoards of the Rosnoën type

Apart from exceptional cases where a cleft in a rock has been used as a hiding place, the treasure is usually deposited in a hole dug in the ground. It may be very carefully constructed—a circle cut out of the subsoil and lined with clay. A flat stone usually serves as a protective covering. The contents may be in a confused heap or laid out in an orderly way; and one cannot exclude the possibility of wooden chests, which have since disintegrated. For example, the hoard at Pennavern, Rosnoën (Finistère)[2] was resting on a layer of black humus, and was protected by two oak beams laid in the form of a cross. In the

METHOD
OF
BURYING
THE
HOARDS

149

Middle Bronze Age a linen bag was sometimes used; at Tréboul, Douarnenez (Finistère), fragments have been found, and some weapons have preserved an impression of the weave in their patina.

Apart from the simple cavity, however, pots occur most frequently as containers. These are often of coarse ware, and of little interest to the chance finder, who used to smash them to get at their contents. Unbroken specimens, therefore, or those which have not 'crumbled into dust', are extremely rare; of more than 50 pots recorded, no more than half a dozen survive. The vessel from Kerguérou, Rédéné (Finistère), containing a hoard of the Late Bronze Age, is a small flat-based crucible. One has heard of hoards of the Late Bronze Age having been found in pots with globular bodies. The one from Vern, Moëlan (Finistère), is of a type that directly recalls certain Urnfield forms. Finally, hoards of socketed axes have been found in pottery imitations of situlae (Kerhon, Roudouallec, Morbihan; Bogodonou, Meilars, Finistère), or even in an actual situla of bronze (Kerléonet, Spézet, Finistère). Some hoards of socketed axes have been found in a circular cavity, with a metal thread passing through the ring of each axe; strips of leather or material may also have been used in this way.

In about 100 Armorican hoards where the mode of conceal-ment is known, there are 53 pots, one linen sack, 19 carefully built cavities, one hoard beneath a wooden structure, and 15 beneath stones.

These hiding places were often situated near landmarks—natural stone blocks or megaliths. In some examples the hoard is actually inside a megalithic monument. In such cases, it may be difficult to tell whether it is actually a hoard or the grave-goods of a secondary burial. Collections of this kind are often atypical; nor must it be forgotten that the Gallo-Romans re-utilised the Passage and Gallery Graves, and may have used bronze, for example, in the form of rings or depilatory tweezers.

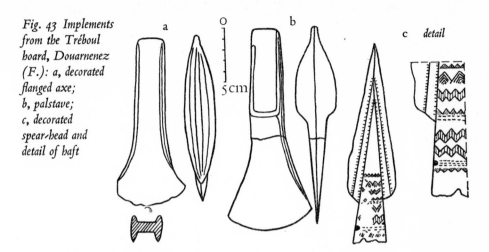

Fig. 43 Implements from the Tréboul hoard, Douarnenez (F.): a, decorated flanged axe; b, palstave; c, decorated spear-head and detail of haft

It is a strange fact that Armorica, which possessed with its Barrow culture one of the largest Early Bronze Age centres, has hardly produced any hoards dating from this period. A few flat axes were hidden during this epoch, and also gold objects, which will be discussed later. Some Early Bronze Age articles such as the crutch-shaped pin from Tréboul, Douarnenez, are found in hoards of the Middle or Late Bronze Age. Mention should be made also of isolated objects such as the dagger with a cylindrical base and rivets from Paimboeuf (Loire-Atlantique), or the tanged sword from Le-Pilon, near Nantes (Loire-Atlantique).

With the Middle Bronze Age period, hoards became larger, and a study of them makes it possible to distinguish between the different chronological periods. The flanged axe makes its appearance, to be supplanted in turn by the palstave. The sword with a broad base and hollow cylindrical hilt succeeds the triangular Armorican daggers. The decoration of the weapons

THE
CHRONO-
LOGY OF
THE EARLY
BRONZE
AGE
HOARDS

Plate 25

MIDDLE
BRONZE
AGE
HOARDS

151

is geometrical, making use of the broken line, chevrons, and hatched zones—motifs which may be emphasised by dotted lines. Finally, towards the end of the period, new types of weapons and implements appear.

The flanged axe was already found in Early Bronze Age barrows, but in the hoards the flanges are more pronounced and the axe longer. The large hoard of Tréboul has produced some fine examples;[2] some are decorated on the sides with concentric ribs. The cutting edge is more splayed than in axes from the Médoc region. These objects are never provided with a lateral loop. Sometimes a dividing line marks off a primitive stop-ridge, or again, the rims may become indistinct and diverge from the sides, meeting to form a rough indication of a round stop-ridge. Axes with a median constriction are rarely found.

Palstaves are quite often found in association with flanged axes. The most primitive specimens are broad, and have no lateral loop (Tréboul, Douarnenez). But the classic axe of the Middle Bronze Age in Armorica is fairly narrow (the median section is almost square). The flat side has a median rib, but in addition one sometimes finds a trident or some more varied decoration on the stop-ridge, as on the axes from the region near the mouth of the Seine. Axes with and without a lateral loop occur together in the same hoards. Sometimes they have been deposited in large numbers (360 at Calorguen, Côtes-du-Nord). The distribution of palstaves is fairly homogeneous in Brittany. Taking only the hoards into consideration, a slightly greater density is noticeable in the southern regions—Loire-Atlantique and Morbihan. Otherwise it will be seen that the whole territory was occupied, without there being any more marked localisation in the interior or along the coast.

Fig. 44 Sword with hollow metallic hilt from the hoard of Le-Castello, Saint-Brandan (C.-du-N.). $\frac{1}{6}$

The swords of the fully-developed Middle Bronze Age have a broad base and a hollow cylindrical hilt. The hoard of Le-Castello, Saint-Brandan (Côtes-du-Nord), contained 8 blades, hidden beneath a stone. These swords are sometimes decorated, as at Tréboul, with geometrical designs on the hilt. The blade has fine incised lines parallel to the cutting edge, no doubt executed with the aid of some kind of fork or comb. At Plougrescant (Côtes-du-Nord) an enormous blade was found, 66½ cm. long and 18 cm. broad at the base of the hilt; this was probably a ceremonial weapon. These swords derive from the triangular daggers of the Bronze Age barrows.

The spear-heads of the fully developed Middle Bronze Age have fairly broad barbs at the base. The socket may be decorated with geometrical designs (Tréboul, Finistère; Maroué, Côtes-du-Nord). The holes for the rivets or pins which secured the shaft are irregular, sometimes bevelled. The barbs are often reinforced with two heavy ribs, sometimes accentuated by parallel lines.

In addition to the weapons, the characteristic Middle Bronze Age bracelets occupy an important position. In most cases these are found isolated or in a special hoard; they are very rarely found in association with other objects. They are heavy bracelets of solid metal, semicircular or rectangular in section; a number of variations exist. The geometrical decoration is produced by checkering and chiselling.

During the Middle Bronze Age an evolution takes place: little by little the palstave supplants the flanged axe, and lateral loops make their appearance. Hoards are found containing axes alone ('merchants' hoards'). Finally, new types replace the earlier ones (such as in the hoard of Pennavern, Rosnoën).[2] The swords are rapiers, and the hilt, of organic material, is fixed to a terminal 'tongue' either by rivets or bands; in the latter case, notches on the tang provide a firm hold. In association with these swords one finds spears with long sockets. Razors with cleft blade and tang are now also used, and various tools—socketed hammers, gouges—make their appearance, announcing the Late Bronze Age, where these

Fig. 45 Massive open bracelet adorned with checkerwork, from Teillay (I.-et-V.). ⅓

153

implements become plentiful. Very occasionally, one finds axes with median wings, such as those belonging to northern Alpine regions.

LATE
BRONZE
AGE
HOARDS

Fig. 46

During the Late Bronze Age the evolution continues with the appearance of swords with tangs provided with slight rims. The hilt is always attached with rivets, the holes for these passing through the core. The palstave continues in use, but is more massive and often has a heavy median rib on the flat sides. The swords have blades which widen towards the end, and are decorated with parallel grooves (pistil-shaped blades). The guard, at first half-cylindrical, evolves towards a V-shape. Finally, little notches (*ricassi*) below the guard protect the hand from cuts. The sheaths have lozenge-shaped bronze chapes at the end.

The advances in metallurgy made possible a much wider range of implements, such as knives, chisels for wood, and nails; attention was also turned to articles of wear—buttons, pieces for appliqué, and belt-plaques.

ATLANTIC
FACIES OF
THE LATE
BRONZE
AGE

Fig. 47

Among the hoards dating from the end of the Bronze Age is a group found in a fairly wide Atlantic area, which was given the name 'carp's tongue complex' by the British writers who first observed them.[3] They are mainly distinguished, in fact, by the presence of swords whose blades narrow suddenly like the tongue of a carp; but there are other characteristics which mark out the complex better—for example, the frequency of axes with sub-terminal wings, which, except in this type of hoard, are very rarely found in Brittany.

Swords and axes are accompanied by a certain number of typical implements; first, small hog-backed knives, with a hole at the back for suspension. These implements are made with re-worked fragments of sword-blades. Bugle-shaped objects, formed of a hollow stem with a loop at one side, are also

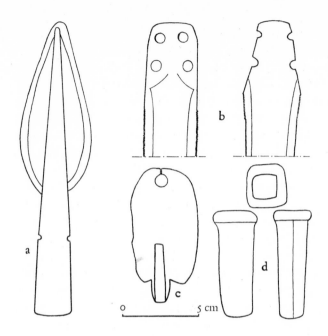

*Fig. 46 Implements
from the Pennavern
hoard, Rosnoën (F.):
a, spear-head with long
socket; b, swords with
tangs, rivets or notches;
c, razor with cleft blade
and tang; d, socketed
quadrangular hammer*

characteristic of this group, though their use (as bits or scabbard loops?) is uncertain. Triangular knives, knives with cleft blade, razors—also cleft and tanged—and ribbed bracelets are common. Swords are chiefly characterised by large rectangular notches below the guard, and a blade with parallel edges, with a considerable mid-rib. There are abundant winged axes; palstaves are rare, and socketed axes are of various types, but always thick and functional.

It was formerly suggested that these hoards are the traces of invaders (the so-called 'Sword-Bearers') coming from the north-west of the Alps to conquer the Atlantic regions. It now seems more probable that this group developed out of local Middle Bronze Age industries. The geographical distribution of hoards of this type in Armorica shows a definite localisation along the coasts, and many have been found on the islands (Belle⁄Ile and Groix, Morbihan; Guennoc, near Landéda, and Ile⁄de⁄Batz, Finistère; Jersey and Alderney).

There seems to have been considerable commercial activity at this period; and a great many objects have a distant origin— for example, the palstave of an Iberian type, with two lateral loops from Le⁄Folgoët (Finistère), or the axe of a Sicilian type, with a vertical hole for the haft, from Nantes; also the bracelet with large tabs, from Ile⁄Verte near Ile⁄de⁄Batz (Finistère)—a Belgian type. Influences from the English Late Bronze Age and from the French Hallstatt (Iron Age) cultures are also discernible; but the relationship most often found is with the Urnfield culture (we have seen that the hoard from Vern, Moëlan—definitely an Atlantic type—was contained in a pot of the Urnfield type). Moreover, there are traces of Urnfield penetration into Brittany not only in Bronze Age material of an Atlantic facies; for example, certain isolated objects such as the sword with a solid hilt from Saint⁄Aubin⁄du⁄Cormier (Ille⁄et⁄Vilaine), a type frequently found in regions influenced by the Urnfield culture.[4] The interpenetration of the two series of industries is, however, not so marked as in the hoards found in central France, where one finds the meeting place of Atlantic elements, travelling up the main rivers, and elements connected with the Urnfield culture.

THE
HOARDS OF
ARMORICAN
SOCKETED
AXES

Attention was drawn to the axes with square sockets, peculiar to Armorica, at an early date. At first, writers des⁄cribed them by various names, since terminology was still fairly imprecise. Their attribution to the Gaulish period—even to Gallo⁄Roman times—qualified them in addition as Celtic; and all kinds of fantastic functions were assigned to them, such as tent pegs or the ends of metal⁄shod sticks. The accumulation of fresh discoveries, and comparison with similar implements, have made it possible to identify them as socketed axes.

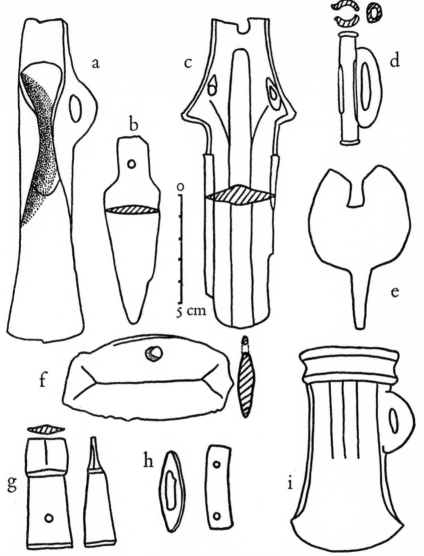

Fig. 47 Characteristic objects of the Late Bronze Age of Atlantic facies: a, winged axe of the hoard from Vern, Moëlan (F.); b, tanged knife of the hoard of Pont-er-Vil, Locmariaquer (M.); c, carp's tongue sword of the hoard of Plouénan (F.); d, bugle-shaped object from the hoard of Pont-er-Vil, Locmariaquer; e, cleft razor from the hoard of Saint-Grégoire (I.-et-V.); f, hog-backed knife from the Menez-Tosta hoard, Gouesnach; g, socketed knife with cleft blade from the Menez-Tosta hoard, Gouesnach; h, ferrule of a sword hilt from the Pont-er-Vil hoard, Locmariaquer; i, socketed axe from the hoard of Kerc'hleus, Saint-Pabu (F.).

Hoards of these axes are plentiful in Armorica; they have yielded far more implements than any other kind of hoard. Statistics should always be accepted with caution; the figures are often exaggerated or unknown. Nevertheless, it is estimated that out of 388 Breton hoards, about 188 have yielded exclu/sively Armorican socketed axes. This gives us about 20,000 implements, taking into account hoards discovered during the last 150/200 years; earlier finds and those which have yet to be made may perhaps double this figure. The total weight of metal used in the socketed axe industry is somewhere in the order of 10 metric tons. By comparison, the Middle Bronze Age in Brittany has only yielded about 1,800 palstaves, representing less than one ton of metal.

It will be seen, therefore, that during the transitional period between the Bronze Age and the Iron Age, industry in Armorica was in full production. The urge for productivity even resulted in the employment of less and less stable alloys, in which lead came near to preponderating.

We will just recall a few details concerning the way the articles were hidden; the radial arrangement of the large hoards, for example, with the axes in several circular layers, the cutting edges towards the centre. They may also be found lying 'head to tail', or thrown in haphazard. The axes may be strung together by a thread passing through the lateral rings. Finally, the smallest hoards are in pottery vessels or, very occasionally, bronze ones.

From the typological point of view, the axe with a square socket is evolved from functional round/socketed types. Little by little, the tendency is towards a non/functional type: the socket is rectangular, the cutting edge is not clearly defined, the walls are often very thin—sometimes even with gaps. In other cases the use of lead produces badly/made and mis/shapen specimens, some with the socket choked up with metal.

A second evolution resulted from reduction in size, producing dwarf or 'votive' forms; the smallest are those from MauredeBretagne, which are 5 cm. long. In the course of this transformation, forms were at first produced which could still be used (as chisels for wood), but the final products were curiosities whose use is problematical.

Fig. 48

The decoration of the Armorican socketed axes is geometrical and fairly simple. On objects which are still functional,

Fig. 49

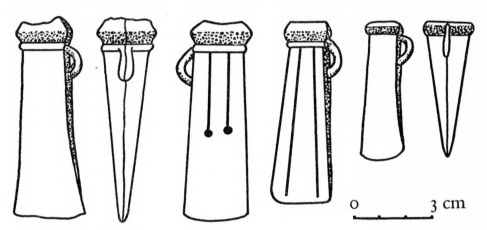

O ⎯⎯⎯⎯ 3 cm

Fig. 48 Types of small Armorican socketed axes

one finds vestigial 'wings', suggested by two semicircles in relief, opposite one another, continuous or dotted. The most highly schematised wings are on one of the axes in the hoard from Lanvaïdic, PortLaunay (Finistère), where they are simply indicated by a cross. Otherwise, decoration is reduced to parallel lines beneath the rim, or vertical lines ending in globules or single, double or dotted circles. Globules are set two, three, four or five together. In some cases this decoration is placed near the cutting edge. A chevron design on the small axes perhaps recalls the median rib of the palstaves.

To what use the axes with quadrangular sockets were put is extremely uncertain. We have seen that some of them may indeed have served effectively as axes or chisels. In the case of specimens unfit for any practical use, it has been suggested that these may have served as currency in commercial transactions. This theory seems to be supported by the fact that their variations in weight seem to be fairly regular. Multiples and sub-multiples have sometimes been found. Moreover, in some hoards the sockets are often full of little fragments of lead, bronze or tin, that could have been added as a make-weight in measuring. There are some axes of bronze, or bronze and lead, which have been cast without a hollow socket; these are simply small metal ingots, also of use in bartering.

Fig. 50

The geographical distribution of socketed axes almost completely covers the Armorican massif. They are particularly dense in the northern areas, from the Manche to the Côtes-du-Nord departments (Manche ranks first with 74 hoards, containing 8,500 Armorican socketed axes); like southern Finistère, Loire-Atlantique has the lowest total (though the figures given below could perhaps be slightly increased):

Ille-et-Vilaine:	18 hoards with		5,500 axes
Côtes-du-Nord:	69 ,,	,,	6,100 ,,
Finistère:	72 ,,	,,	7,100 ,,
Morbihan:	23 ,,	,,	1,700 ,,
Loire-Atlantique:	6 ,,	,,	80 ,,

Outside Armorica, the square-socketed axe was widely distributed in the Atlantic region. It is found in a few hoards in the Midi, Gironde and Charente, in the south of England, in Belgium, and as far afield as Germany.

From the chronological point of view, it is difficult to obtain precise information, because so few exact associations are known. It occurs with palstaves in some hoards of the Atlantic type; but the most interesting association is that with iron articles (a small ingot at Saint-Martin-des-Champs, Finistère), indicating a fairly late date. In some Gaulish cemeteries (Kerviltré, Saint-Jean-Trolimon, and Saint-Urnel, Finistère) socketed axes or fragments of them have been found, but we

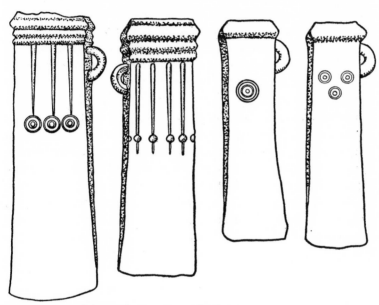

Fig. 49 Types of decorated Armorican socketed axes. ½

cannot tell whether these were functional or obsolete. It therefore seems that this industry must have survived for a fairly long period, after the end of the true Bronze Age.

More gold objects dating from the Bronze Age have been found in Armorica than in any other part of France. Some small ornaments of this precious metal were already included in the grave-goods of the Passage Graves, coupled with the

GOLD
JEWELS
FROM THE
BRONZE AGE

Chalcolithic complex. The first series of Bronze Age barrows, and also (less frequently) the second series, contain gold too, particularly in the decoration of dagger hilts. In the course of the Middle and Late Bronze Age the graves disappear, and one only finds isolated articles, or objects in hoards. Unfortunately, they are very rarely found in association with dateable bronze objects; moreover, one must beware of re-utilisation, or of inherited 'family jewels' found in a late context.

Fig. 51

The lunulae imported from Ireland are now generally attributed to the Early Bronze Age. They have been found in two localities of the Côtes-du-Nord; one at Saint-Potan, and a larger treasure trove from Kerivoa, Bourbriac. This consists of a beautiful lunula, two smaller ones, a small head-band, and two fragments of wire torques with flat terminals, similar to the one found at Arlon (Luxembourg).[5] The lunula from Saint-Potan (like the three found long ago in Manche) was not accompanied by any other object.

The gold ring-disc from Maël-Pestivien (Côtes-du-Nord), found in association with two bronze ingots, is also usually attributed to the Early Bronze Age. Some authors have related it to the solar symbols of the Late Bronze Age; but its simplicity, its similarity to the ring-discs made of fine types of stone, and the proximity of the lunulae, suggest rather that it belongs to the Early Bronze Age, since the interpretation of all ring-discs as solar symbols remains valid.

From the Middle Bronze Age onwards, an increasing variety of forms is found. There are torques formed of a ribbon of metal twisted in a spiral, with hooks at the ends (Abbaretz, Loire-Atlantique). A more complicated variant has several spirals: there is a collar from near Quimper (Finistère) with five such, ending in two hooks. But the most beautiful specimens of the Late Bronze Age are the torques (of the Yeovil type) made of a twisted rod, cruciform in section, ending in hooks with conical swellings. The one from Cesson (Ille-et-Vilaine),

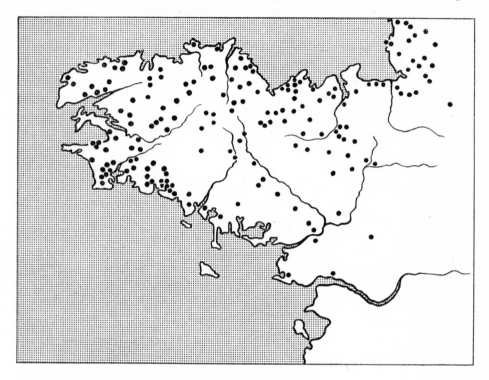

Fig. 50 Distribution map of hoards of Armorican socketed axes

found coiled in a spiral, measures 1 m. 40 cm. when it is extended, and weighs 389 g. (12·5 troy ounces). But that from Plouguin (Finistère) must have been still finer, with a total length of
1 m. 48 cm. and weighing 456 g. (14·6 troy ounces).

There are some massive torques decorated with checkered
patterns which must also be attributed to the Middle Bronze
Age, or even to the end of the Early Bronze Age. One of them
was found with other bracelets and spiral ear-rings (the
treasure of Collédoc, Vieux-Bourg-Quintin, Côtes-du-Nord).
The other is from the Iron Age cemetery of Kerviltré, Saint-

Fig. 52

Jean-Trolimon, but this association is not very convincing, as fragments of swords of the Middle Bronze Age were also found amongst Iron Age articles. A similar torque was found in Vendée (Massigny). These three torques are very like the decorated gold bracelet from the well-known barrow of Leubingen (Saxony), of the Early Bronze Age. A torque from Keryéven, Loqueffret (Finistère) is of a much simpler type, hexagonal in section and with slightly trumpet-shaped ends.

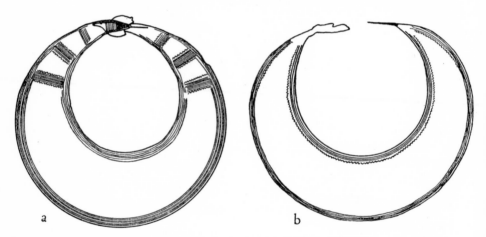

a   b

Fig. 51 Gold lunulae from: a, Saint-Potan (C.-du-N.); b, the hoard of Kerivoa, Bourbriac (C.-du-N.). Both ¼

Fig. 53

In addition to the torques, some bracelets have also been found. Practically all of them are of the penannular type, and usually thickened at the ends. The main part of the bracelet is either cylindrical in section or flat and ribbon-like; a few specimens are semicircular in section. They are seldom found in association with bronze implements. However, at Martigné-Ferchaud (Ille-et-Vilaine), a bracelet was found together with a palstave, and at Collorec (Finistère), two others accompanied some Armorican socketed axes. It is probable, therefore, that they were first used in the Middle Bronze Age, and persisted down to the Late Bronze Age—no doubt even later. They are not decorated, except in the case of a flat bracelet from the Matignon hoard (Côtes-du-Nord), which has a line of chevrons near the opening. Their weight varies from 30 to 200 g. (1 to 7 troy ounces), according to type. Those from Collorec both weighed more or less the same—45 g. 635 and 46 g. 685 (1·467 and 1·5 troy ounces) respectively, which implies fairly exact means of measuring.[6]

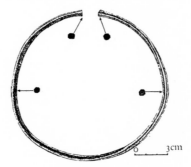

Fig. 52 Gold torque from Keryéven, Loqueffret (F.)

Besides necklaces or bracelets, fragments of plaques are sometimes found, decorated with repoussé work (Lanrivoaré, Finistère), and little coiled ear-rings (also at Lanrivoaré). Finally, at Coët-Correc, Mur-de-Bretagne (Côtes-du-Nord), some bronze spear-heads contained in their sockets a spindle-shaped bead, a piece of a thin gold plaque, and two little rings.

Of course, a great many early discoveries are unavailable to us, because they were immediately melted down. Sometimes a drawing or cast survives; but in most cases the memory of the hoard is all that remains.

None of these objects has been properly analysed; most have been tested by the touchstone method. The majority are proba-bly a natural mixture of gold and silver, with the quality reduced to the level of 'electrum' (more than 25 per cent silver). There may often be a local origin for the precious metal; traces of gold have been found at a number of points in Brittany, and not so long ago gold-washers were operating in the beds of some rivers. But most was perhaps imported. In the Chalcolithic period, gold articles seem to have been concentrated on the south coasts, which suggest an Iberian origin. The lunulae certainly come from Ireland, and so do the spiral torques. As for the bracelets, both Galicia and Ireland are possible sources; but the largest hoards of bracelets are found on the English Channel side.

THE LATE
BRONZE
AGE
DWELLING-
PLACES

Although the hoards are almost our only source of information for the Middle and Late Bronze Age, some traces of dwellings have been observed which may belong to the latter phase. Near the find-sites of hoards it is not unusual to pick up fragments of pottery or flint flakes—the meagre traces of a period of occupation. Sometimes rather larger relics have been found. At Questembert (Morbihan), near a hoard of Atlantic type, there were fragments of wattle, made of baked clay and still bearing the impression of the branches and logs forming the walls of the dwelling; also a piece of pottery with rough excised decoration (a series of oblique lines), a coarse jar filled with roasted acorns, and finally pieces of a quern for grinding corn.

The La-Torche peninsula, Plomeur (Finistère), contained a dwelling-place which was in use from the Neolithic to the Iron Age. Some articles from the Bronze Age level have been collected: a tranchet knife, a hog-backed knife, a spear-head, and a bronze pin, accompanied by fragments of coarse pottery decorated at the edge with finger impressions. At Saint-Pabu (Finistère), objects of Atlantic type are found amongst bones of pigs and horses, and a few human remains.

The site on the Roc'h-an-Evned promontory, Ploubazlanec

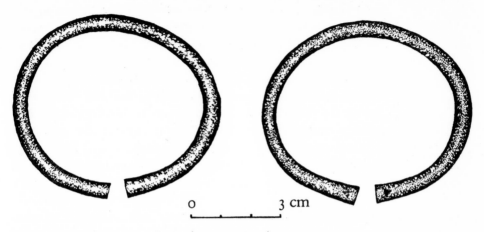

Fig. 53 Penannular bracelets of gold from Rungallic, Collorec (F.)

(Côtes-du-Nord),[7] must also belong to the Bronze Age. This promontory, at the mouth of the River Trieux, near Loguivy-de-la-Mer, occupies a commanding position. On the side nearest the river, the cliff is very steep and the approach extremely difficult—as it is also on the flanks, bounded by two equally steep-sided dry valleys. The rear does not have such strong natural defences; here, therefore, the spur has been fortified with an earthwork, now between 1 and 2 m. high and 5 to 6 m. wide. On the outside, the embankment is faced with small vertical stones, and bordered by a small ditch 1 m. 20 deep, hollowed out of the rock but partially filled in. Originally, the system of defences must have comprised a main section about 60 m. long and very wide, and two additional sections protecting the flanks. Excavation of the embankment shows that it consists of a clayey silt, brought from some 200 m. away.

The material collected from under the earthwork is fairly meagre—flint flakes, and pieces of broken pottery. There are three varieties of the latter: firstly, buff fragments, coated with a slip, of fairly large vessels—a kind of variant of Late Neolithic pottery; secondly, fairly fine pieces, dark red, well fired, belonging to pots which had probably been made on a slow wheel, with little oblique incisions beneath the rim and in the interior. The third type is slipped, fine, and very hard. This group may belong to the Late Bronze Age, but the absence of other similar materials makes precise dating very difficult.

METAL-
LURGY OF
THE
BRONZE
AGE IN
ARMORICA

We have, in fact, very little information on this subject; no workshop, nor any trace of how the metal was obtained. However, the founders' hoards provide evidence of a flourishing artisan industry. Crucibles are very rare, but cakes of metal reproduce their internal shape; they were small and hemispherical, with a pouring spout. The mould plugs and the metal castings show that the molten metal was poured into bivalve moulds (the line of separation of the valves can be seen on axes). Some clay moulds have been found (Plumieux, Côtes-du-Nord; Pennarven, Hanvec, Finistère). At the end of the Bronze Age, bronze moulds are common; they have been found, for example, at Dinard (Ille-et-Vilaine), Groix (Morbihan), and Mellac (Finistère). They must have served as prototypes for the clay moulds. The sockets of the axes have in many instances preserved traces of clay matrices. Wood may also have been used, as can be seen from certain impressions inside the hilt of a sword from Tréboul, Douarnenez.

Metal was often transported from place to place in the form of cakes. Some of these are of copper, and therefore cannot be the result of melting down worn bronze objects. They formed the smith's reserve of metal; and some hoards consist entirely of such cakes (Tourch; Kerlaz; Plonevez-Porzay, Finistère).

It is difficult to establish any precise origin for the ore, because almost all of it must have been obtained by surface working: skimming the top of a lode, or washing coastal or river sediment, But exploitation was probably local, and this is no doubt one of the causes of the rapid spread of the Early Bronze Age Armorican barrows; after having worked the coastal alluvium (first series of barrows), the prospectors may have penetrated further inland to look for more promising deposits, along the rivers and through the natural gaps indicated by the distribution-maps. In this way they would have reached the metal-bearing regions south of the Monts d'Arrée and near Huelgoat, where silver, lead and a little copper may have induced some populations to settle for a while. Subsequently, the search must have become general throughout the peninsula. No doubt tin played an important part, and the presence of stone or bronze axes on the stanniferous lodes of La Villeder (Morbihan) and Abbaretz (Loire-Atlantique) may not be fortuitous. But there are no traces of extensive exploitation any earlier than the Gallo-Roman period,[8] and maps showing the distribution of various Bronze Age objects do not reveal denser concentrations near these lodes. The only known case of exploitation is that of Donges (Loire-Atlantique), where, on the Ile d'Er, 40 socketed axes were found which had the same composition as the ore from a near-by mine, the Pont-du-Gué: lead with traces of iron not exceeding 1 per cent.

A series of petroglyphs engraved on isolated blocks, or on rocky outcrops, which have sometimes been thought to be symbols of the Christianisation of pagan places, belong to the family of the so-called prospectors' signs, found from Galicia to Eire.

The simplest of these signs is the cup-mark, which was widely used at various periods. On some rocks, the little cup-marks are grouped irregularly (Penhoat, Saint-Coulitz, Finistère; Roh-Priol, Quiberon, Morbihan). But usually they are accompanied by more typical, if enigmatic, designs. Cruciform figures are obtained by joining the cup-marks with perpendicular lines, but these may be Christianisation signs

(Gueradur, Pleumeur-Bodou, Côtes-du-Nord). Dotted circles (Kerpenhir, Locmariaquer, Morbihan), and particularly concentric circles (La-Roche-Méha, Pleucadeuc, Morbihan, unfortunately destroyed) are very close to the Irish engravings of Cork and Kerry, and to the Spanish engravings in the province of Pontevedra. Several stones in the Guérande region (Loire-Atlantique) resemble rocks in Galicia; at Méniscoul, Piriac, the most frequent sign is a kind of cross, sometimes surmounting a rectangle, while at Brandu, La-Turballe, the finest design is a quadruple quadrilateral with a cross superimposed, one of the arms of the latter ending in an ellipse. Finally certain representations of human feet are perhaps connected with the same group of signs (Roh-Priol, Quiberon; more hypothetically, the feet added to the engravings of the Petit-Mont Passage Grave, Arzon, Morbihan).

In Ireland and in Galicia, one tends to interpret these signs as reconnaissance marks of mining districts, the metal in this case being copper and, in Galicia, tin as well. It is possible that in Loire-Atlantique and Morbihan these inscriptions are also prospectors' marks, the metal sought being tin, lead and gold. Be that as it may, these petroglyphs provide fresh evidence of the close cultural relationship between the Atlantic provinces in the north of Portugal, Galicia, the Vendée, Brittany and Ireland.

CHAPTER X

The Armorican Iron Age Cultures

IT IS PROBABLE, though not certain, that the first infiltra-
tions of people bringing with them the Urnfield traditions
and then the Hallstatt culture corresponded at least in part with
populations speaking a Celtic language. They might, indeed,
equally well have been people impregnated by certain aspects
of the material culture of the Celts, through the rather dense
screen of the pre-Celtic populations of western and central Gaul
at that period—even, in part, through the occupants of some
regions of Aquitaine or even Spain.

One cannot rely on the sole toponymic record to have sur-
vived more or less directly from the periplus of the Carthaginian
Himilco, *c.* 500 B.C. (known to us chiefly through a document
of Rufus Festus Avienus, A.D. 370), who referred to the famous
Cassiterides as *Oestrymnis* or *Oistrumnis*. This is certainly a pre-
Celtic term; but since the islands in question are variously
located by scholars in the Iberian peninsula, Armorica and the
British Isles, this information is of limited value.

But the Massaliote Pytheas, who set sail in about 320 B.C.
(known to us chiefly through Strabo, A.D. 19) already testifies
definitely to the existence of a Celtic place-name *Uxisama* for
the island of Ouessant, among pre-Celtic names such as
Corbilo, Kabaion and *Ostimii* or *Ostidamnii* (probably a corrup-
tion of *Osismi*). It is not long before the whole company of
classical authors (Julius Caesar, Pomponius Mela, the elder
Pliny and Ptolemy) give us more ample information regarding
the names of the peoples and places of Armorica.

Of five Gaulish tribes who occupied the end of the peninsula,
the names of two are certainly pre-Celtic (*Osismi* and *Coriosolitae*), the affinities of two are less certain (*Namnetes* and
Veneti), and one is perhaps Gaulish (*Redones*: cf. Gaulish *reda*,

chariot). The place-names show a mixture of pre-Celtic and Celtic terms, the latter predominating. *Sicor* and *Corbilo* are pre-Celtic. *Condate, Icoranda, Brivates (Portus), Uxisama, Vorgium, Gesocribate, Vindana (Portus), Vindilis (Insula),* and *Condevincnum* are Celtic. The name *Darioritum* is probably half Celtic.

Some names mentioned only in more recent periods, such as names of rivers (the Vilaine for instance), also seem to be autochthonous pre-Celtic survivals.

One may conclude from this that during the Iron Age, and especially during its later phase, groups of people arrived in Armorica who spoke a Celtic language and christened a good many places and regions, but who did not come in sufficient numbers to supplant the earlier inhabitants, still less to exterminate them—if indeed there were conflicts. This agrees to some extent with the conclusions of archaeology, which establishes that in spite of the fame of some Armorican tribes (particularly the Veneti) they have left very little material evidence apart from hill-forts and coinage, and one is therefore inclined to the belief that most of the population was content with a very simple mode of life, only faintly reflecting the brilliant Celtic culture of the continental regions.

VANGUARD INFILTRA-TIONS OF THE FIRST IRON AGE In its regional individuality, the end of the Armorican Bronze Age seems to have dragged on for a considerable time, in a state of industrial stagnation, during the whole of the First Iron Age (the Hallstatt period), so that the latter is, so to speak, hardly represented at all. This epoch is characterised by nothing more than a few indications of commercial influences or infiltrations from the more continental regions of Gaul. There are comparatively rare imported objects; articles of Late Bronze Age types, in which the new techniques developing elsewhere with the first Iron Age cultures have been adapted to the Armorican taste, are relatively more plentiful in some parts of Armorica, even taking into account lacunae due to our imperfect knowledge of the central region and the northern coasts.

We have seen that during the last phase of the classical Late Bronze Age, or Proto-Hallstatt II (900-750 in eastern Gaul), corresponding to phase III of the Urnfields (Hallstatt B) and to the first appearance of the use of iron, there were some isolated arrivals in Armorica of peoples related to the Urnfield cultures.[1]

For the moment, there is nothing definite that corresponds with Hallstatt I (750-600 B.C.; Hallstatt C); a few importations, all very late and probably already overlapping the early La Tène period, and found in isolation, can be attributed to Hallstatt II (600-500 B.C.; Hallstatt D). An iron sword with antennae, 94 cm. long, with fine lines engraved on the blade, has been found in the Donges marshes (Loire-Atlantique); it has a square tang with bronze discs at the end of it, terminating in antennae with knob decoration. An iron sword, of a rare type, comes from the Goulaine marshes, Pont-de-l'Ouen (Loire-Atlantique); it has two round knobs on the guard, a flat tang widening in the centre, and four knobs on the hilt (a similar sword comes from Néau, Mayenne).

It is striking to find all these objects together in the Loire estuary or its neighbouring marshes, following the numerous Late Bronze Age swords also dredged from the river bed. It is tempting to suggest a connexion with the pre-Roman tin route, which was supposed to run up the Loire, starting at Corbilo (a pre-Celtic place-name) at the mouth of the Loire, joining the Seine towards its source, and used in addition to the route that followed the Seine alone down to the Channel, the better to enable Massaliote merchants to break the Punic blockade of the Maritime Atlantic route.

While the expansion of the Iron Age culture in western Europe is largely linked with the progressive spread of waves of

Celtic invaders—or, at least, in the case of outlying regions like Armorica, with their partial infiltration, coupled with that of the native populations in Gaul which had already undergone Celtic influence—we still have no trace in western Armorica of any real 'Celticisation' of the population during the whole of the First Iron Age, nor perhaps even during the early years of the Second. In fact, everything which seems to belong to the Hallstatt period is really late Hallstatt (also called prolonged Hallstatt) or Post-Hallstatt, dating from the early La Tène period, after 500 B.C.

THE LATE HALLSTATT ROUND BARROWS The classic Hallstatt barrows of eastern Gaul, notably those of Burgundy and Franche-Comté, do not extend beyond the centre of France, at the most. Generally speaking, the Hallstatt barrows in Gaul are distributed in the south-eastern half of the country, corresponding with regions mostly over 200 m. above sea-level. The most recent ones, in the Pyrenees or Aquitaine, have been influenced by Urnfield traditions lingering on, and contain mostly incinerated remains. All types quite often have circular internal walls.

Fig. 54 With this tradition can be linked a series of barrows in Morbihan and southern Finistère, having a quite possible connexion with Aquitaine; they are commonly known as 'circular graves' because of their internal dry stone construction.[2] They are 10 to 20 m. in diameter; their average height is between 1 and 2 m. The outer construction is of earth. The circular wall, about 1 m. high and averaging 5 to 6 m. in diameter, is built of a regular series of schist slabs, in the shape of a cylinder or of a truncated cone, trimmed only on the outer face. Inside, one sometimes finds pits, dug in the ground, or little cists of simple slabs, possibly superposed, containing cinerary urns. One already begins to find from time to time small stelae or 'betyls' in the form of spherical domes, ovoid shapes, or rough pyramids.

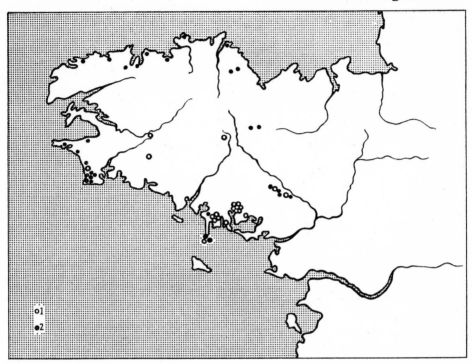

Fig. 54 Distribution map of cremation tombs of the Iron Age: 1, late Hallstatt circular graves; 2, long barrows and sunken tombs

The urns in these monuments are very characteristic. In one of the circular graves found at Le-Rocher, Le-Bono (Morbihan), a situla of plain sheet bronze was found, banded with iron but with handles and rivets of bronze; this vessel had for a lid a hemispherical bowl, upturned, made of bronze, its edges adorned with a line of S-signs. The pottery urns mostly have 'metallic' shapes, recalling round-bodied prototypes such as the preceding example, or carinated ones. The base is usually flat, sometimes umbilicated in the centre, and there may be a pedestal; the neck is straight with a curved rim, except in the

Plates 60-62

175

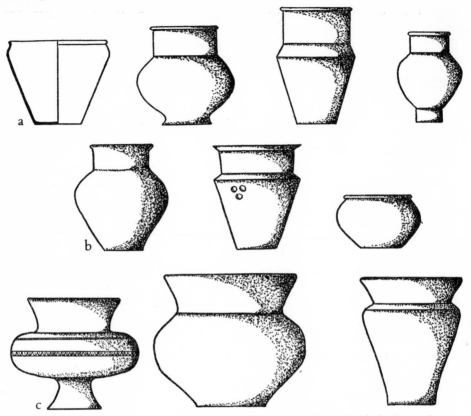

Fig. 55 Cinerary urns from: a, the circular grave of Boquidet-en-Sérent (M.); b, the circular graves of Nignol and Coët-a-tous, Carnac (M.); c, the Roz-an-Trémen cemetery, Plomeur (F.). All ⅛

squatter shapes. The micaceous paste of these pots is well fired; the surface is lustrous, brown or more often black, with a brilliant graphitic slip applied which accentuates the 'metallic' appearance. These pots are decorated only with cup-marks on the body, either individual large ones (Coat-Penn-Coat, Saint-Goazec, Finistère), sometimes with nipples in the centre (La-Bourlaie, Pleucadeuc, Morbihan), or groups of three small ones (Coët-a-tous, Carnac, Morbihan). The beaded rim is already found at Boquidet, Sérent (Morbihan). *Fig. 55*

The cinerary urns usually had a plaque of schist or granite as a lid, instead of being covered by another vessel turned upside down (like the situla from Le Bono, and cinerary urns from various regions).

The other grave-goods, present only in the series of eleven barrows found at Le Rocher, Le Bono, consist of the ornaments belonging to the deceased: simple bracelets of bronze or iron, characteristic bracelets with bosses or globular nodes on the outer circumference, bronze 'pinion-wheel' bracelets, and in the only tomb where inhumation had taken place, 24 bronze and two iron bracelets, of which 18 were made in two parts and fastened by tenons at the end of the movable segment which dovetailed into the main section; finally, bracelets of lignite and schist, either barrel-shaped or flat and decorated with incised lines and *dents-de-loup*; also rings, nails, remains of weapons, and beads of blue glass.

Fig. 56 Bracelet of bronze with bosses, in two parts, from the circular grave of Le Rocher, Le Bono (M.). ¼

There remains a series of monuments whose date is uncertain because of very meagre grave-goods and the absence of characteristic structures. The *grées* or plateaux in the interior of the Morbihan region of eastern Brittany, and in central Brittany, provide numerous examples of groups of small barrows, consisting simply of a heap of stones. These have produced scarcely anything, on the original ground level, beyond bits of wood, charcoal, flint flakes, fragments of quartz or pieces of broken pottery which could belong either to vessels of coarse ware from the end of the Bronze Age or to types which may date from the beginning of the local Iron Age.

THE GROUPS OF SMALL BARROWS *Fig. 57*

The smallest of these are hardly more than a metre or two in diameter; most are somewhere between 3 and 7 m. across, and some are as much as 15 m. in diameter; but none are more than about 1 m. high. A barrow of this type on the Grée de Carate,

M

Pluherlin (Morbihan) has been dated by the radio-carbon method to 450±60 B.C.

In a few exceptional cases, they have produced some glass beads, one ribbed (Saint-Colombier, Sarzeau, Morbihan), or bronze 'pinion-wheel' bracelets, with knobs and with the ends meeting, or closed and with hollow egg-shaped or spherical balls of a fair size. Taken all in all, these objects are of the same type as those from the circular graves.

THE CRE- MATION CEMETERIES Apart from natural cases of regional backwardness, the circular graves may be taken to date from what is known as the La Tène period (Second Iron Age), though till now they have only produced goods from the end of the First Iron Age or articles common to that period and the Second Iron Age.

The graves belonging to this period—apparently the oldest— still have Hallstatt traditions, and are cremations in urns of very similar shape to those of the circular graves; they are usually grouped in little cemeteries—a kind of late 'Urnfield' on a small scale.[3] Instead of an urn, there is sometimes a small cist built of a few slabs of rock. Both kinds of cinerary container often occur side by side (Roz-an-Trémen, Plomeur, Finistère); sometimes one even finds pots enclosed in cists (Lannvréon, Peumerit, Finistère).

Fig. 54 These cemeteries may be actually in the ground, or in small circular or elliptical barrows. In either case, they may include one or more funerary stelae. The barrow at Lannvréon, Peumerit, was an ellipsoidal mass of stones measuring 12 by 4 m.; that of Kerancoat, Ergué-Armel (Finistère), was sub-circular, with an average diameter of about 11 m.; it was 1 m. 20 high, and contained three stelae, each surrounded by four urns. One of the stelae was quadrangular, the other two cylindrical. The cemetery of Kerviltré, Saint-Jean-Trolimon (Finistère), must have covered an oval measuring 40 by 30 m., containing at least five granite stelae; one of these had four faces

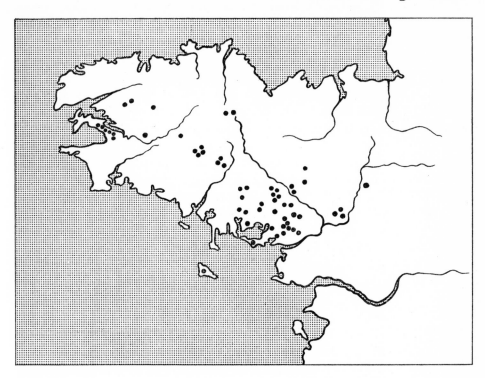

Fig. 57 Distribution map of the small barrows and groups of smaller tombs of the Iron Age

and four grooves at the angles, one had seven sides, and two had longitudinal ridges (15 on one of them). The cemetery of Roz-an-Trémen, Plomeur, was spread over a wide area; it was split up into nuclei grouped round at least six granite stelae, two of which were fluted.

There are, as we have seen, examples of granite stelae in Armorican Iron Age cremation cemeteries, both in the circular graves (Boquidet, Sérent; La-Bourlaie, Pleucadeuc; and Le-Rocher, Le-Bono), where the stones are roughly hemispherical, ARMORICAN GAULISH STELAE AND THE BETYLS

179

and in the apparently more recent cemeteries mentioned above. They also occur in sites where the end of Gaulish independence and the start of Roman occupation are both represented (Kerhillio, Erdeven, Morbihan), the stones being roughly hemispherical. [4] But they are prevalent (always of granitic rock) throughout Lower Brittany, either in isolation, or as re-used by the Romans (the famous stela of Kervadel, Plobannalec, Finistère, for example, with sculptured representations of seven divinities), and particularly by the Christians—which has given rise to many controversies regarding the exact age of these monuments (on which 'Celtomaniac' archaeologists have bestowed the misleading name of *lec'h*).

Nearly all these stones are cut to a regular shape, symmetrical about a vertical axis, the diameter decreasing towards the top. The height (without reckoning the rough-cut base intended to be embedded in the ground) varies from 30 cm. or so to about 3 m. The top may be cut off flat, or rounded and merging gradually into the body of the stone. The stone may be circular in section (in imperfect specimens ovoid or elliptical) or polygonal; quadrangular, often with the corners rounded or cut off, sometimes emphasised by grooves; hexagonal, heptagonal, decagonal, or with an even greater number of sides. In some cases the lines of intersection of the plane surfaces may be curvilinear and the outline globular. Those of circular section may be decorated with grooving or mouldings, contiguous or separated by fillets; in this case they are simply a variation of multiple polygonal facets. It is, of course, difficult to establish a rigorous geometrical classification for these monuments, because there are transitional forms of all the different kinds, from the large fluted shaft in the shape of a truncated cone to the low spherical dome-shaped stone. One often finds cup-marks on these monuments, especially on the top of the latter type— usually only one, but sometimes several. A few large stelae are cut with several deep grooves at right angles to the axis, which

Plate 68

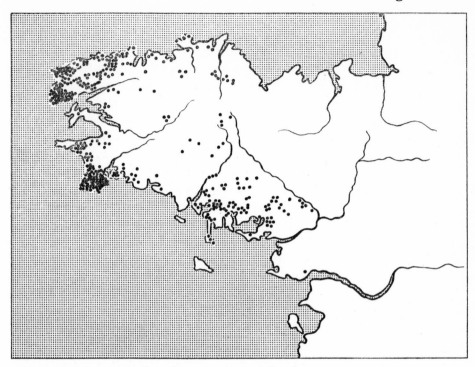

Fig. 58 Distribution map of upright Armorican Gaulish stelae

may have resulted in breakage (as with a stela at Kerviltré): this
is probably the effect of much later sawing attempts.

If one makes a rough typological division of these stones into
two series—those of a squat shape, approximately hemispherical
and those that are of an upright form—one discovers that their
geographical distribution, although it overlaps completely,
shows that the zones of concentration of the two types differ.
The hemispherical stelae, which are closest to the similar
stones of the circular graves, are very numerous in Morbihan,
and less common in Finistère and Côtes-du-Nord. The tall
monuments, on the other hand, are in general more evenly

Figs. 58, 59

distributed, but the smallest are mostly in Morbihan and the largest in Finistère; the latter are particularly plentiful in Bas-Léon and Basse-Cornouaille.

The interpretation of these stelae, so varied in their morphology, is not very easy. Where they are found in cemeteries, this certainly points to their having been used for specific funerary purposes; but their subsequent re-utilisations suggest traditions which attributed more general functions to them. Archaeologists have been somewhat too ready to assume that the upright stelae are derived from the menhirs; another explanation had to be found for the hemispherical stones, these having been construed as miniature symbolic versions of barrows or as phallic symbols—in a few cases the latter seems more likely.

Some of these stelae are really betyls, with sculpture or stylised ornamental engravings. The most celebrated is that of Kermaria, Pont-l'Abbé (Finistère), 50 cm. high from the base up, roughly quadrangular, with a Greek key pattern and a frieze of double-S spirals framing four different cartouches. One of these contains a swastika with the arms bent from right to left, another is a square divided by eight radial lines, another has four leaves or tear-drops, and the fourth is of more complex design. A fragment of a cylindrical stela which broadens slightly towards one end, from Tréguennec (Finistère), has alternating Greek key designs and double-spiral friezes; and the piece from the top of a similar small stela from Kerru, Ploaré (Finistère), has a frieze of chevrons. The stela from Sainte-Anne, Trégastel (Côtes-du-Nord), quadrangular with truncated angles, has the remains of a characteristic engraving in the middle of one side—a motif of vertical double spirals, framed between two grooves.

STATUARY The ornamented stelae which have just been discussed are granite versions of decorative sculpture found in the early Celtic art of countries as far apart as the Rhineland and Ireland.

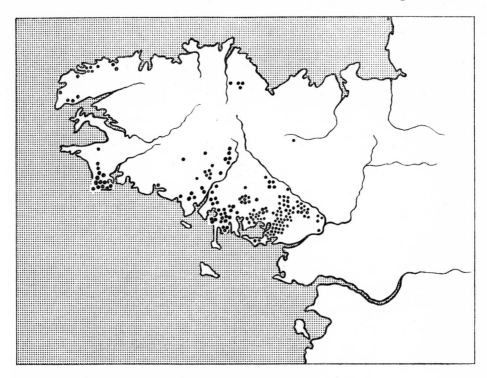

Fig. 59 Distribution map of low (hemispherical) Armorican Gaulish stelae

Gaulish sculptured figures are very rare in Armorica. At the most, one can probably attribute to the beginning of the independent period a crudely-carved granite statuette from Lanneunoc, Plounevez-Loc'hrist (Finistère).[4] The head has disappeared. The torso, oval in section, is 60 cm. high, with no trace of legs. A slight ridge divides the lower part. The shoulders are very square; the arms are held close against the sides, with the forearms horizontal; the hands, no doubt clenched, are almost touching. The thumbs are clearly indi-cated, and are raised dagger-like, as on many Armorican

Plate 69

Gaulish coins. The head is clearly differentiated from the bust, but the neck is scarcely indicated.

Even during the Roman occupation, there was little sculpture, perhaps because the available stone was so difficult to work. The Gaulish tradition shows itself in the god with a mallet from Rillan, Saint-Brandan (Côtes-du-Nord), in three groups of a rider overthrowing a monster with a snake's tail in place of legs—the so-called 'anguipede'—(evidently late in inspiration, and from far away), and in the Romanisation of the conical Gaulish stela from Kervadel, Plobannalec, with four sculptured panels at its base, depicting five divinities, a child, and an animal in bas-relief. Like the Christianisation which many of these Gaulish stelae also underwent much later, this shows how they continued to have significance for the population long after the Roman conquest.

INHUMA-
TION
CEMETERIES
Inhumations are often found amongst the cremations in cemeteries from the beginning of the Second Iron Age (Kerviltré; Roz-an-Trémen), and in such cases it is rare for the funerary ornaments of the dead to show any notable difference in date.

However, in addition to the more or less isolated tombs, there are also large inhumation cemeteries. In every case, these cemeteries are found in littoral regions, amongst the dunes of calcareous sand; elsewhere, the bones have not been preserved. It is impossible to say whether such cemeteries could have existed in the acid ground of the interior without leaving any traces, or whether they were only established in sandy ground because it was so much easier to dig graves under those conditions.

Fig. 60

Some of these cemeteries were in use for very long periods, with a stratigraphy of successive tombs keeping pace with the accumulation of the dune. This applies to the enormous necropolis of Saint-Urnel, Plomeur (Finistère),[5] where hundreds of

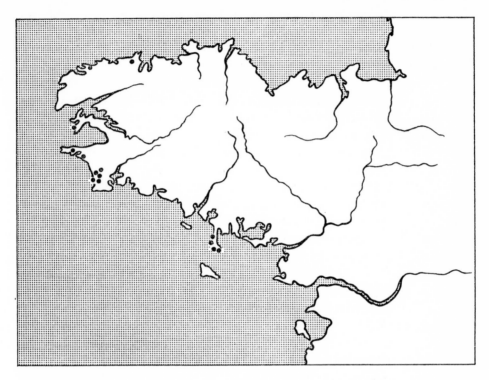

Fig. 60 Distribution map of the flat cemeteries with inhumations, all interstratified in sand dunes

bodies were buried. The lack of any grave-goods makes a
precise dating impossible; but the fragments of articles found
in the bottom strata, which is of more earthy consistency, indicate that it is not earlier than the transition stage from the First
to the Second Iron Age, whilst those scattered at the top
suggest that the cemetery continued in use until the beginning
of the Roman occupation. The other inhumation cemeteries, in
particular those in the dunes of the peninsulas of Crozon
(Finistère) and Quiberon (Morbihan), belong to the very end
of Gaulish independence and the first century of the Gallo-

Roman period. In these one sometimes finds cinerary urns from this latter period.

A separate trench was dug for each body (often destroying, disturbing or cutting through underlying tombs), and was usually surrounded with a rectangle of small slabs set on edge (or sometimes laid flat, in dry stone construction); there are often one or two larger slabs at the end near the head. At Saint-Urnel the tombs sometimes had a dressing of small pebbles on the top. Most of these graves are orientated east-west, the head towards the west. The bodies usually lay on their backs; if the trench was too short, head and feet were propped up against the ends. Arms and hands lay straight down alongside the body, or the hands were crossed on the abdomen. At Roz-an-Trémen, there were instances where the body had been tied with the thighs crossed, the legs being parallel. Occasionally the body is found curled up or in a crouching position. In some instances, at Saint-Urnel, two adults were laid one above the other in the same grave. Young children were buried more or less anyhow.

Incidentally, it should be noted that in the cemeteries of Saint-Urnel, and Lostmarc'h, Crozon, there were examples of extensive cicatrised trepanning.

MATERIAL EQUIPMENT OF THE SECOND IRON AGE

Whether it comes from graves, from isolated finds, or from areas where traces of occupation have survived, the equipment found in Armorica presents a very incomplete picture of the material culture of the period.

Weapons and tools are very rare. The physico-chemical nature of the soil is certainly unfavourable to the preservation of articles made of iron; and once they have deteriorated—however little—it becomes extremely difficult to distinguish between Gaulish and Gallo-Roman articles.

A few noteworthy items provide evidence of Italian importations. Thus, at Rennes, a belt-clasp of cast bronze was dis-

covered, very close to an original type dating from La Tène I—
a unique specimen on this side of the Rhine. The oppidum
of Tronoan, Saint-Jean-Trolimon (Finistère), where properly
conducted stratigraphical excavations would no doubt have
produced usable industrial series before the total devastation of
the site, has yielded up some fragments of a helmet, dating from
La Tène I, of an Italian or Italo-Greek style; it is made of iron,
covered with bronze foil with repoussé decoration, and has a
terminal boss of coral and a cheek-piece of iron covered with
bronze.

Iron swords of the La Tène type are rare. Two or three have
been found in the Loire, at Nantes or in other places of Loire-
Atlantique. The oppidum of Tronoan has produced a whole
range of swords, but their condition makes it difficult to distinguish between Gaulish and Gallo-Roman. There is certainly a simplified anthropoidal sword among them.

The pseudo-anthropoid dagger found at Le Faou (Finistère),[6] with iron blade and tang, and the hilt and sheath of
bronze, decorated in high relief, with chape only very slightly
convex, was at one time taken for a Celto-British or even an
Irish weapon imported during the Roman period. More recent
studies have shown that it is a round-headed variant of a type
of dagger of the La Tène III period, with definite Roman
influence, but probably dating from the time when Gaul was
still independent.

The iron knife found at Quiberon, in the mound of
Kernavest, dates fom La Tène I; its sheath is wood, plated
with three sheets of bronze, richly decorated geometrically with
interlaced half-circles, concentric circles of dots, triangles and
lozenges. It was probably placed in the tomb long after it had
been made. Lances with indented blades have been recorded
(Gaulish or Gallo-Roman), notably at Toul-Bras, Quiberon.

However, apart from a few stone objects of commonplace
types, found at all periods of proto-history, including pebble-

tools (some pebbles being used as sling-stones), spindle-whorls, weights or pendants, and a few crude flake-tools, and excluding the pottery, which will be discussed later, the commonest items are articles of attire or ornamental objects.

A belt-clasp of bronze, of very simple design, found on a child's skeleton at the bottom level of the Saint-Urnel cemetery remains an isolated example.

Fibulae, which are particularly characteristic objects for distinguishing between different periods, are all too few. The most interesting specimens are the iron fibulae, in cross-bow form and with the foot bent up at right angles, ending in a knob; a specimen was found in one of the urns from the Kerancoat cemetery, Ergué-Armel, and another, possibly two, in urns from the Roz-an-Trémen cemetery, Plomeur.[7] These fibulae are typical of post-Hallstatt graves in the north-west of the Iberian peninsula, the cemeteries of the Pyrenees and of Aquitaine; a few specimens have also been found in Cornwall. The fibulae which are really typical of La Tène I are found, either entire or very much damaged, in cinerary urns from several Finistère cemeteries (Bagatelle, Saint-Martin-des-Champs: four of iron and one of bronze; Roz-an-Trémen, Plomeur: two of iron; Lannvréon, Peumerit: fragments of an iron specimen); there is also a fibula of decorated bronze, of a local type, belonging to the same period, from Commana (Finistère). The fibulae of La Tène II are only known to us through three iron specimens from the cemetery of Tronoan, and one of bronze from Corseul (Côtes-du-Nord). The La Tène III fibulae are fairly frequent in the mixed Gaulish and Gallo-Roman cemeteries such as Kerhillio, Erdeven, and Kerné, Quiberon (Morbihan), the oppidum of Tronoan, Saint-Jean-Trolimon, and the site of Trez-Goarem, Esquibien (Finistère).

Bracelets of lignite (the material for these probably came from Switzerland) or of black schist (perhaps from the Naqueville

workshop near Cherbourg, Manche) are still found in a fragmentary state, notably in the adventitious burials of the
Morbihan megaliths. A wooden bracelet or ring was found in
the Kerviltré cemetery, Saint-Jean-Trolimon. Here there was
also a bronze armlet with bosses, its two ends touching, and
simple bronze bracelets resembling those found in the inhumation cemeteries of Quiberon in association with simple iron
bracelets. Glass bracelets, often polychrome, are found in late
cemeteries such as that at Kerhillio, Erdeven, and in the hoard
at Brech (Morbihan) which dates from after the Roman conquest.

Necklace beads, whose date is uncertain when they are
found in isolation, are fairly common; such trinkets could
easily be exchanged by stages over long distances. Cornelian
specimens have been found, often with geometrical facets—
one in the mound of Saint-Colombier, Sarzeau, two in a tomb
at Plobannalec, and a number in tombs at Plonevez-Porzay
(Finistère). Amber beads have been found in the tomb at
Saint-Galles, Arradon and in the Brech hoard; a lignite bead
also comes from the Saint-Galles tomb.

Blue glass beads are more plentiful; they have been discovered in the Kerviltré cemetery, Saint-Jean-Trolimon, the
dwelling-site of La Torche, Plomeur (some with white equa-
torial incrustations), and the mound of Saint-Colombier,
Sarzeau. The beads of the late La Tène III hoard of Brech are
polychrome.

Fortunately, sherds and even entire pots are plentiful and
varied, and therefore provide easier chronological landmarks
than the other articles. Two large families of pottery can be
distinguished, and are in the main successive.

First of all, we find a continuation and development of the
pots of 'metallic' shapes which we have already encountered in
the late Hallstatt circular graves, and which are the most

THE
GAULISH
POTTERY
OF
ARMORICA

Plates 63–67

Fig. 55

typical cinerary urns in the cremation mounds and cemeteries. A larger variety of types is encountered, some of them extremely elegant in shape.

In addition to the black or grey pastes with a lustrous and graphitic surface which predominated in the circular graves, brown and micaceous pastes are often found, covered with a slip of haematite, producing a beautiful brownish-red colour only found in Armorica and in the south of Britain, but linked with the Hallstatt tradition of red-painted pots.

All these urns may have incised linear or curvilinear decoration, which is also found in the following series: pots from the mound of Lann-Tinikei, Ploëmeur, and from Kergonfalz, Bignan (Morbihan); from the cist at Kerbascat, Tréguennec, extraneous to the circular grave in the same place; urns from
Figs. 55, 61, 62
the mound of Lann-vréon, Peumerit, and the cemeteries of Kerviltré, Saint-Jean-Trolimon, and of Roz-an-Trémen, Plomeur. These designs are sometimes copied from metalwork motifs, with characteristic stippled backgrounds, or again
Plate 66
with dotted circles; more often with rows of imprinted crosses, Greek keys and other motifs—the most famous being the sloping S-shaped signs where it is not very difficult to recognise stylised friezes of little ducks or waterfowl, and which are also encountered in the civilisation of the post-Hallstatt *castros* of Galicia and the north of Portugal, or in the Cornish forts.

Painted cinerary urns are very rare, since the only one we know is the magnificent specimen constituting a secondary grave on the top of the Kergourognon barrow, Prat (Côtes-du-Nord), whose lid is an upturned bowl, also painted.

This first group of pottery, on account of its association with the cremation it contains and because of the other indications of date, can be attributed to La Tène I and II, if indeed these subdivisions have any real meaning in Armorica. In any case, it is never properly speaking turned on a wheel, and it has a great many affinities with post-Hallstatt cultures.

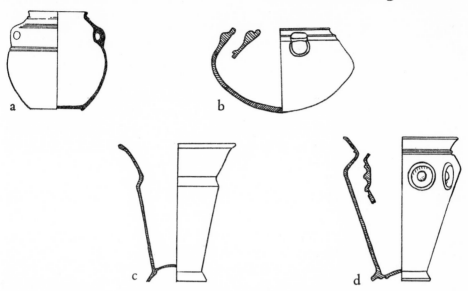

Fig. 61 a, Pot with countersunk handles from Merdiez, Plouzévédé (F.); b,c,d, cinerary urns from the Lannvréon mound, Peumerit (F.): b, imitation bronze cauldron, the suspension rings shown applied; c, carinated pedestal urn; d, pedestal urn decorated with nipples. All ⅛

The second group would then correspond to La Tène II and III. The fine well-fired grey and black pastes with a brilliant graphitic slip not only continue in this group, but here reach their finest development, because they were made on a *tournette* (slow-wheel) or a potter's wheel. At the same time, the forms of the vessels change, probably because they are no longer in general use as cinerary urns but are put to more practical uses— as food containers, for example. These pots also benefit from the style of decoration derived from metal-work, especially motifs with pendentive circles, and concentric dotted circles.

This pottery possesses several individual characteristics. The bead-rims and the internally grooved rims, the counter-sunk handles with the wall of the vessel thickened both internally

Fig. 61a

Fig. 62 *Decorative motifs from the urns of the Roz-an-Trémen cemetery, Plomeur (F.)*

and externally, form close links with pottery from the south-west of the British Isles.[8]

The most regular of these pots are made on the wheel, and probably belong to La Tène III, or even to its continuation under the Roman occupation. The others, carefully modelled, may have been made on the *tournette*.

There is also a very rare series of these pots, richly decorated with splendid designs added to the simpler motifs of the customary types. Stylised palmettes are used as the ornamental theme on the beautiful pot from Saint-Pol-de-Léon, while sophisticated friezes of S forms decorate the Kélouer pot, Plouhinec (Finistère) and some fragments from the underground gallery of Blavet, Hénon (Côtes-du-Nord).

Only a few fragments of painted ware from this period are known in Armorica (from the underground gallery of Ruguéré, Plouvorn, Finistère).

Fig. 63
Fig. 64

Finally, in addition to the regular ones, there is a whole range of pots, no doubt commoner and more utilitarian, often of rather coarse ware full of mica or quartz. These are sometimes turned on a wheel and sometimes modelled; the decoration, when there is any, consists simply of finger-nail impressions on the upper part of the body or incisions on the rims, there being no slip. Countersunk handles, however, occur fairly often.

Fig. 63 Ornament from the Saint-Pol-de-Léon pot

Very few villages have been recorded: groups of rectangular dwellings, probably with very low walls, built of dry stone or pieces of turf. All the known instances are in the interior (Séglien, Melrand, Guern, Morbihan; Brennilis, Finistère), and it is not quite certain that they go back as far as the Iron Age; they could be poor medieval dwellings. OCCUPA-TION OF THE LAND: DOMESTIC SITES

More frequently, fragments of baked clay are found, bearing the imprint of interlaced branches, from wattle which may have formed the walls of flimsy huts. These have often been found in underground galleries or in their immediate proximity, which suggests either that there was a normal dwelling-site near-by, or that the entry to the shelter was surrounded by wattle. Diffuse sites of an earlier date are perhaps a continuation of those of the Late Bronze Age.

Elsewhere, beneath the coastal dunes in various regions, hut floors have been found, round domestic hearths—notably in the late La Tène III sites in Morbihan. Very little definite is known about them from the architectural point of view.

The abundance of querns and mortars provides the most perennial traces of dwelling-sites and the cultivation of cereals. It seems to have been only at the very end of the period of Gaulish independence, at the earliest, that the use of rotary querns for crushing grain is first met with in Armorica.

Beneath the ancient dunes which covered large coastal areas, one finds here and there traces of 'furrows' from early cultivation —a kind of ditch separating parallel beds of old vegetable-fossil soil. Traces of this kind are present notably in Finistère,

Fig. 64 Ornament from the Kélouer pot, Plouhinec (F.)

at Penmarch, Saint-Pol-de-Léon and Plougoulm. In the last-mentioned locality, it has even been possible to follow out the remains of old field-embankments, containing large blocks of stone and a few fragments of Gaulish pottery, which shows how ancient this type of enclosure is in Armorica.

THE UNDER-GROUND GALLERIES

Fig. 65

Little underground galleries and chambers, dug out of the subsoil where this i sufficiently workable, are very plentiful from the Gaulish period in Armorica; they are usually of a different type from the underground refuges or shelters of other parts o Gaul during the pre-Roman period. Moreover, they are only found in the west of Armorica. They are rather

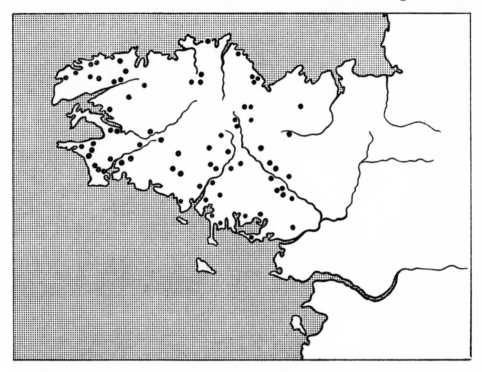

Fig. 65 Distribution map of the Iron Age underground galleries

different from the Cornish *fogous*, which are trenches with walls of dry stone masonry and an artificial covering; and they are also unlike the Irish subterranean chambers, or the underground houses of Scotland.

For a long time they were believed to be graves, because in some cases cremations or inhumations had been found. They may rather have been hiding-places or shelters, with very few objects, which indicates a purely temporary occupation. But they were certainly used by the living; kitchen refuse is found in them, and even hearths with chimneys. Perhaps some served as store-pits.

These cavities are always discovered by accident; there is no indication of their presence above the ground. Usually a farm horse—nowadays a tractor—breaks through the roof of a chamber, and so reveals an excavation which it is often very difficult to explore subsequently; because of the earth which has fallen in, one is never certain of having found everything, or even of having discovered all the 'rooms' on the site.

There may be one chamber only, or several (up to half a dozen), linked by tunnels averaging 35 cm. in diameter, through which it is necessary to crawl, and which open into the lower part of the chamber walls. The first room is reached by a corridor about 50 cm. in diameter, entering the ground at an oblique angle. In one case (Park Rugolven, Primelin, Finistère), the first orifice was sealed with a flat stone laid on edge. The chambers or crypts are often oval or elliptical in shape, and their ceiling generally has the appearance of a rudimentary vault; they may be in a series, one following another, but sometimes the axis of one of them is at right angles to that of the others. They are excavated out of disinte-grated rock, which sometimes bears the marks of metal tools; their size varies between 1 m. 20 and 6 m. in length, 1 m. and 3 m. in width, and 90 cm. and 2 m. in height.

Where traces of goods are found in these chambers, they are usually in the one nearest the entry. In addition to pottery, there may be spindle-whorls, pebble-tools, the remains of iron or bronze articles, and traces of wattle. In one very remarkable instance (Trézéan, Pédernec, Côtes-du-Nord), there were three stelae hidden in chambers; at least one of them, which was too large to bring in through the entrance tunnel, had been inserted through the roof of one of the chambers. Perhaps these stelae had been concealed there after the Roman conquest—possibly during a period of Christianisation. In any case, some under-ground refuges were visited, or even re-utilised, during the Gallo-Roman period, as is shown by various pieces of pottery.

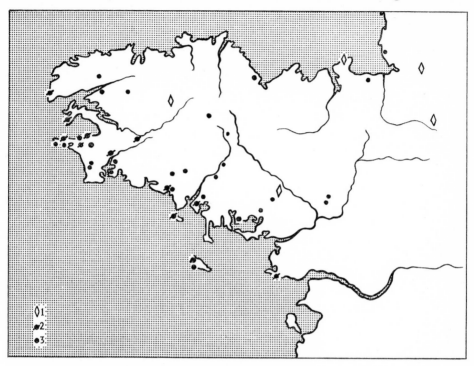

Fig. 66 Distribution map of hill-forts: 1, multivallate oppida with murus gallicus;
2, multivallate oppida with earth ramparts; 3, univallate oppida and forts

The camps, which could be a permanent protection on the OCCUPA-
site of a dwelling or, on the other hand, might only be used TION OF
when some specific danger threatened, increased in numbers THE LAND:
from the Iron Age period. Even in our times there still survive, THE OPPIDA
at least in part, quantities of earthworks for which no precise
date is provided either by their morphology or by the presence
of any objects, and which cannot be attributed with certainty
to the Iron Age, the later part of the Gallo-Roman period, or
even to the Dark Ages, since the traditional *castrametatio* may
have persisted for a long time in Armorica as in other similar

regions—particularly in Ireland, where the 'ring-forts' are very like some Breton 'châteliers', most of which belong certainly to the Dark Ages. To be on the safe side, therefore, we will leave out some of the simple entrenchments on hills, and some of the promontories defended by one line of earthworks and a ditch.

Fig. 66

One can definitely attribute to the Gaulish period the oppida with several lines of fortifications[8]—usually two or three—actuated by the use of the sling as a defence weapon. Circum-vallations of the same type are found in south-west England, especially Cornwall.

Rocky promontories with cliffs rising sheer from the sea, with defences at the point where they join the mainland, are frequently found on the Atlantic coast, and spurs overlooking rivers have been fortified in a similar manner in neighbouring regions. These sites with natural defences have been re-used at later periods, and the remains of superposed medieval struc-tures are often found in them.[9] Early archaeologists frequently mistook medieval pottery for Gaulish ware.

Plate 70

Among the best-preserved sites is that of Lostmarc'h, Crozon (Finistère). The picturesque sites of Koz-Kastel, Beuzec-Cap-Sizun, and Kastel-Meur, Cléden-Cap-Sizun

Plate 71

(Finistère), were re-utilised during the medieval period, but the foundations of the little rectangular Gaulish huts have been found there, on a series of ledges overhanging the sea.[10] The fine site at Kervédan, Ile-de-Groix (Morbihan) was also reconstructed, but at the beginning of our era, so that it com-prises seven successive ditches.

The hill-forts of the interior belonging to this series are less numerous. The finest is the camp at Kercaradec, Penhars (Finistère), with double ramparts. The well-known camp of Péran (Côtes-du-Nord) is rather different; it consists of a double enceinte, with its embankments vitrified, no doubt as the result of a fire which burnt the network of beams supporting the structures. This camp is on raised ground, but is not in a particularly good strategic position.

One is inclined to attribute to the period of the Roman conquest a number of hill-forts, sometimes unfinished, with a *murus gallicus*—a wall of interwoven stones and beams, these fixed to one another by iron nails. The best known is the camp of Artus at Huelgoat (Finistère), which was heightened at a later period and roughly subdivided. The other examples are strung out along the line of retreat of the Veneti, and above all of their allies the Coriosolitae, towards Cotentin and Jersey at the time of the invasion, the camp of Lescouët, Guégon (Morbihan), the Mainga headland, Saint-Coulomb, the oppidum of Le Poulailler, Landéan, in the Forest of Fougères (Ille-et-Vilaine), continuing via the camp of Le Châtellier, Le Petit-Celland (Manche). Most of these fortifications are multiple, at least in part.

The Armorican Gauls certainly extracted and worked iron and tin in the peninsula, at least on an artisan scale; but, whatever may have been said on the subject, there is nothing to justify attributing to them with certainty the traces of early exploitation discovered on the site of some lodes of these minerals, nor the quantities of iron dross and the few iron ingots that have been recorded.

INDUSTRY DURING THE GAULISH PERIOD

In spite of the renown of Armorican tin throughout the antique world, therefore, the old mine-workings of La Villeder (Morbihan) or of Abbaretz and Nozay (Loire-Atlantique) hardly seem earlier than the Gallo-Roman period, in the light of recent researches.[11] These deposits were certainly skimmed on the surface—a process which had begun during the Bronze Age. Moreover, no tin dross or ingots have ever been found in Armorica.

The plentiful heaps of iron dross found throughout the peninsula, where iron ore abounds, do not seem attributable to smiths of a date any earlier than the Gallo-Roman period, or even the Middle Ages. A few iron 'pigs' have been found, in the form of spindle-shaped ingots; but their age is indeterminate, since working by artisans has produced similar objects at all periods.

THE
ARMORICAN
TRIBES
Fig. 67

The area covered by this book concerns only the territory of the five most westerly cities of the Armorican confederation, which at one time reached almost from the Gironde to the Seine. The territorial limits of these tribes[1,2]—still subject to discussion in matters of detail—probably corresponded to those of the Gallo-Roman cities which succeeded them after the Roman conquest (these in turn have largely been determined according to the information supplied by Christian religious history, and the boundaries of the first bishoprics). However, the supposed frontiers are quite well supported by the distribution of the coins found in isolation—that is, corresponding to currency lost within the perimeter of its normal circulation.

From the archaeological point of view, we know nothing of the organisation of the Armorican tribes. Most of the populations must still have been widely dispersed in little villages, living in a very simple and primitive manner, and leaving no traces. As for the agglomerations, particularly those of the city centres, where there certainly must have been solidly constructed buildings, these have left no traces either; we do not even know their exact position. One is led to the conclusion that the Gallo-Roman towns were built on the same sites, and the previous buildings rased right down to their foundations.

So, strange as it seems, the only definite evidence we have regarding the Armorican cities is their coinage. It proves the existence, in each tribe, of an organised central power, with the capacity and means for minting money and regulating its circulation.

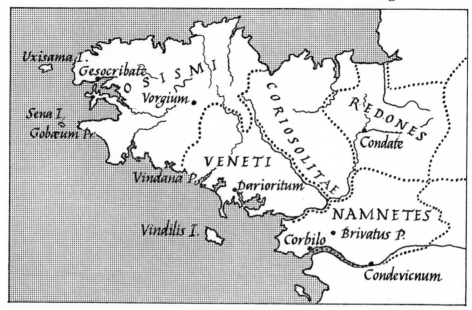

Fig. 67 Map of the Armorican Gaulish tribes

From an early date, and up to about 120 B.C., gold coins seem to have been struck in central Gaul for the requirements of trade.[13] The fall of what has been called the Arvernian Empire resulted in the installation of mints in the large cities, from which the coinage was distributed regionally. In Armorica, this role devolved upon the powerful Veneti.

Although not all the gold coins found in continental Armorica have yet been attributed with certainty to their source, those of the Veneti have been identified. They are very good staters, weighing 7 g. 90 (nearly 122 troy grains), and made definitely convex on the obverse. On this side is a human head of admirable design, though departing to some extent from Greek realism; it is surrounded by beaded cords, ending in little heads. On the reverse, imitation of the Greeks is still very

THE
ARMORICAN
COINAGE

Plate 72

201

much in evidence; a galloping horse figures on it, driven by an auriga, or charioteer, who frequently holds a whip. A figure with outstretched wings usually appears beneath the horse. In the first century, the Veneti issued fine coins of silver alloy, of a pattern analogous to that of the gold coins, and made in exactly the same way.

The neighbouring peoples imitated the money of the Veneti. The Osismi, their neighbours to the west and north, had a gold coinage lighter in weight and of a lower standard. They pro-

Plate 73a, b

gressively debased the metal, which became what is known as electrum (a ternary alloy of gold, silver and copper); but the money of the Osismi contained gold till the Romans came.

The Redones, to the north-east, had gold coins which were also not very distinguishable from those of their neighbours.

Plate 73f

Their silver alloy coins and copper money are well known; their mark is a wheel beneath the horse.

The Coriosolitae, to the north, abandoned numerous hoards of copper money, especially in Jersey; on the reverse, beneath

Plate 73d, e

the traditional horse, there is sometimes a boar and sometimes a lyre.

The Namnetes, to the east, struck a remarkably stable type

Plate 73c

ranging from gold to base silver; on the reverse, a half-length figure with outstretched arms holds the legs of the horse.

THE GREAT
FLEET
OF THE
VENETI

Armorican prehistory ends tragically with the Roman conquest. The most famous episode is the naval battle which recent researches[14] have shown to have taken place off Saint-Gildas-de-Rhuis (Morbihan), and during which the greater part of the Veneti's famous fleet was destroyed in 56 B.C.

We have not yet found any of the Veneti's ships. However, various nautical, archaeological and ethnographical data indicate that the ancestor of the *sinagot*, the fishing-boat of Vannes,

Fig. 68

was a fairly massive construction about 30 m. long, with seamed planking, and about 9 m. wide amidships; it had a draught of about 2 m., the prow and stern were raised, and there was a square cross-jack rigged on the horizontal yard of a central mast. This sail must have been of fine and supple skins, such as parchment. The vessel was navigated by means of steering oars.

Such a vessel was capable of transporting a fairly large cargo, and the commercial importance of the Veneti, famous in

Fig. 68 Reconstruction of a vessel of the Veneti

antiquity, was perhaps founded more upon their command of the sea than upon the rich products of their country and the size of their towns.

It may be that the real 'barbarians' were not those to whom that name is generally applied. We do not know if the Armorican cities suffered as cruel a fate as that meted out by Latin ferocity to the survivors of the Veneti, thus crippling a complete and original Armorican civilisation.

As we have seen throughout this book the Armorican peninsula experienced a continual shifting of influence—in turn continental and maritime, northern and southern, Nordic and Mediterranean. It absorbed into itself both peoples and the most intangible cultural contributions, yet staunchly preserved a regional culture with its own individual and independent characteristics.

From Protohistory to History

We have no precise information as to the situation of Armorica during the first period following Caesar's campaign. It seems that Celtic coins remained in circulation, since there were late issues of small standard size, and that coins of eastern Gaul made their appearance, in consequence of the upheaval. A few articles or a few coins discovered here and there testify thereafter to the beginnings of a progressive Romanisation, which asserts itself above all during the second half of the first century. The expedition of Claudius against the British Isles, which increased commercial activity and perhaps led to the construction of the first important road, brings Armorica into the general evolution of Roman Gaul and of the Roman world.

Without attaining to the prosperity and the splendour of the towns and settlements of those parts of Gaul that came within the orbit of the Mediterranean, or of the military garrisons along the barbarian borders, the material culture of Armorica was far more developed than is generally realised, flourishing at least into the third century.

The system of roads, established gradually, was quite important, linking towns whose more spectacular monuments have largely disappeared, but which nevertheless included important buildings and covered wide areas. Towns like Rennes (*Condate*), Corseul (*Fanum Martis*), Coz-Yaudet, Ploulec'h (*Vetus Civitas*), Carhaix (*Vorgium*), Douarnenez, Quimper (*Aquilonia*), Vannes (*Darioritum*), Nantes (*Condevicnum*), among others, have yielded valuable archaeological evidence, in spite of wholesale destruction or pillaging over the centuries. Certain ports must have been quite active, especially on the Loire near Nantes, or at Douarnenez. Large estates and isolated rural establishments were numerous and situated on well-favoured sites; a Mediterranean style of living, characterised by such luxuries as baths, facings of imported marble and so forth, testifies to the wealth of the owners. The peasants, on the other hand, of which we have few traces, must have had widely scattered and poor habitations.

As the third century progressed, a period of general insecurity set in, as evidenced by hoards of coins and the building of a complementary road system. The larger towns (Rennes, Vannes, Nantes) were fortified, garrisons were established all over the country, while a network of camps and guard-houses was organised to complete the country's defence—hitherto uncalled for, it would seem.

But the repeated expeditions of the Saxons, who systematically devastated the Armorican seaboard and contributed to the undermining of the Empire, mark the beginning of a period of progressive decline in the peninsula. Nearly all the buildings in the towns and outside show signs of fire and sacking; indeed, it has been stated that at the beginning of the fifth century, the two-thirds of the population succumbed, though this may be an exaggeration.

Christianity had nevertheless taken root. As early as the fourth century bishops had sees in Nantes, Rennes and Vannes. One is even led to wonder whether there were not already bishoprics further to the west, and whether most of the inhabitants of those parts were not by this time Christianised.

The second quarter of the fifth century sees the beginning of the emigration of the Britons from Britain, where the pressure of the Saxons, who were now settling there, became more and more oppressive. The result was the emigration of these Britons to western Armorica, gradual but continuous up to the beginning of the seventh century. As early as by the end of the sixth century, the land is called *Britannia*, Brittany.

Very little is known of this period. In the absence of historical sources we have to rely on the more or less legendary lives of the British and Irish Saints who accompanied or preceded the immigrants. Here we have protohistory with practically no archaeological evidence. It is reasonable to assume that the newcomers did not always settle in without clashing with the inhabitants of the country, who were more numerous than has frequently been assumed. The struggles of Waroch around Vannes are evidence of that, as was the mass conversion of peoples described as pagan.

The furthest extension of the Bretons towards the east occurred as late as the ninth century, when they infiltrated into the marches where the last archaeological and toponymic evidence of the Merovingian influence fades out, having really never penetrated into Breton-speaking Brittany.

Practical Information

The best time of the year to visit Brittany, with a view to seeing its monu‑ments and its museums, is either just before, or just after, the tourist season proper—namely, during May, June, September. Less favourable, though still feasible, would be October and the early part of July.

The principal prehistoric monuments fall into the category of Historic Monuments and are protected; some are even owned by the State. In the area under consideration they are administered by the *Conservateur Régional des Bâtiments de France* at Rennes; the *Architectes Chefs d'Agences des Bâtiments de France* (at Quimper, Vannes and Rennes), together with the *Architectes* and *Architectes‑en‑Chef des Monuments Historiques*, are responsible for their maintenance.

French law strictly regulates archaeological excavation, in order to safeguard the national archaeological heritage, which in the past has too often been violated by unqualified and irresponsible persons. Nobody is allowed to excavate without permission from the *Ministère de l'Education Nationale*, even on his own ground, and all such work must be con‑trolled by the *Directeur de circonscription archéologique* (*préhistorique* where the period up to the Bronze Age is concerned, *historique* for Celtic and Gallo‑Roman antiquities). Every archaeological discovery, whatever the circumstances, must be notified to these, and the local, authorities.

The principal collections of archaeological material found in Brittany, both prehistoric and protohistoric, in order of importance, are the *Musée des Antiquités Nationales* at Saint‑Germain‑en‑Laye (Seine‑et‑Oise), the *Musée Préhistorique Finistérien*, Saint‑Guénolé‑Penmarch (Finistère), the *Musée Archéologique* of the *Société Polymathique du Morbihan* at Vannes, and the *Musée J. Miln – Z. Le Rouzic* at Carnac (Morbihan). Lesser public collections are to be found in the museums of Rennes, Dinan, Saint‑Brieuc, Morlaix and Nantes (*Musée Archéologique départmental*), whilst the collection of the *Laboratoire d'Anthropologie* at Rennes is available, on request, to specialists. There are no longer any private collections of note. But, outside Brittany, valuable material is to be found in the museum at Le Mans (Sarthe), at the British Museum and the Ashmolean at Oxford.

Notes

Chapter II

1 Giot and Bordes, *L'Anthropologie*, 59, 1955, p. 205.
2 Gruet, *Bull. Soc. Préhist. Fr.*, 54, 1957, p. 397.
3 Laplace-Jauretche, *Bull. Soc. Préhist. Fr.*, 54, 1957, pp. 422 and 534.
4 M. and S.-J. Péquart, M. Boule and H. Vallois, *cf.* Bibliography, 1937.
5 M. and S.-J. Péquart, *cf.* Bibliography, 1954.
6 Giot, *Bull. Soc. Préhist. Fr.*, 44, 1947, p. 116.

1 *See* De Laet, *The Low Countries*, London, 1958, pp. 59, 71 and note 2 on chapter IV, p. 177.
2 Godfray and Burdo, *Bulletins of the Société Jersiaise*, XV, 1949, p. 21.
3 In French archaeological literature, the western Neolithic of most of France has been called, in recent years, 'Chasséen', but this term has of late been discountenanced (*cf.* Escalon de Fonton, *Bull. du Musée d'Anthr. Préhist. de Monaco*, no. 2, 1955, p. 243; Audibert, *Bull. Soc. Préhist. Fr.*, 55, 1958, p. 94). Moreover, the 'Chasséen' pottery of Brittany being very different in aspect from that of the sedimentary basins of France, the present authors have preferred, in their own recent French publications, to call it the local '*Néolithique Primaire*' (that is, the local Neolithic I, or Neolithic A); but owing to the different semantic use of the words 'primary' and 'secondary' in English archaeological literature, these terms cannot be used in this translation.

   For general reference to Neolithic cultures in France, *cf.* Piggott, *L'Anthropologie*, 57, 1953, p. 401, and 58, 1954, p. 1; Bailloud and Mieg de Boofzheim, *Les civilisations néolithiques de la France dans leur contexte européen*, Paris, 1955. Though very valuable, these two general works are already out-of-date.
4 In his paper of 1954 (*cf.* note 2), Piggott puts all the channelled ware in his 'Chalcolithique', equivalent to our Late Neolithic culture; but he includes in it the false channelled decoration of the Conguel type.

5 Giot and L'Helgouach, *Annales de Bretagne*, 62, 1955, p. 55, and 63, 1956, p. 22.

6 Le Rouzic and Péquart, *Carnac, fouilles faites dans la région, campagne, 1922*, Nancy, 1923; Piggott, *Antiquity*, 1937, p. 441; Jacq, *Gallia*, 5, 1947, p. 162.

7 It is impossible to refer here to the numerous descriptions or excavation reports of Breton Passage Graves.

For the classical Morbihan area, note throughout: Le Rouzic, *L'Anthropologie*, 43, 1933, p. 225, and 44, 1934, p. 485.

8 Giot and L'Helgouach. *Bulletin Soc. Archéo. Finistère*, 81, 1955.

9 Giot, *Gallia*, 14, 1956, p. 189, and 16, 1958, p. 123; *Antiquity*, 32, 1958, p. 149; Giot and L'Helgouach, *Bull. Soc. Préhist. Fr.*, 53, 1956, p. 326, and 54, 1957, p. 358; *Annales de Bretagne*, 64, 1957, p. 9.

10 M. and S.J. Péquart and Le Rouzic, *cf*. Bibliography, 1927. Breuil, Le Rouzic and Boyle, *Préhistoire*, 6, 1938, p. 8. Breuil, *Préhistoire*, 13, 1959.

11 Giot, *Bull. Soc. Préhist. Fr.*, 56, 1959, p. 292.

Chapter IV

1 *cf*. Briard and L'Helgouach, Bibliography, 1957. *cf*. also Hatt, *Bull. Soc. Préhist. Fr.*, 53, 1956, p. 434.

2 Giot, Briard and L'Helgouach, *Bull. Soc. Préhist., Fr.* 54, 1957, p. 493; *Gallia*, 16, 1958, p. 67.

3 In addition to those mentioned in the text: RocherJacquot, SaintGermainenCoglès (IlleetVilaine); Kerandrèze, Moëlan; Lesconil M. Plobannalec (Finistère); Kerlagat and Lizo, Carnac; LannBlaën, Guidel; Kergazec, Plouharnel; Pontivy (Morbihan).

4 Le Rouzic, *Revue des Musées*, 5, 1930, p. 169.

5 Briard and Giot, *L'Anthropologie*, 60, 1956, p. 495, and 61, 1957, p. 167. Briard and Maréchal, *Bull. Soc. Préhist. Fr.*, 55, 1958, p. 422.

Chapter V

1 In their recent French publications, the authors of this book have preferred to call these Late Neolithic Cultures the local '*Néolithique Secondaire*' that is, the local Neolithic II, or Neolithic B), but owing to the application of the words 'Secondary Neolithic' in recent

English archaeological literature, these expressions cannot be translated adequately here. *cf*. Giot, L'Helgouach and Briard, *Bull. Soc. Préhist. Fr.*, 55, 1958, p. 270.

2   General paper by Childe and Sandars, *L'Anthropologie*, 54, 1950, p. 1.

3   Le Rouzic, *cf*. Bibliography, 1930. The plates give the false impression that many of the vase-supports are preserved; in reality there are only very small sherds.

4   Gaudron, *Bull. Soc. Préhist. Fr.*, 43, 1946, p. 302. Fournier, Giot, L'Helgouach and Sieveking, *Bull. et Mém. Soc. Emulation Côtes-du-Nord*, 85, 1956, p. 1.
    Few authors believe in the Nordic connexions of these pots.

5   M. and S. J. Péquart, *L'Anthropologie*, 45, 1935, p. 369; Le Rouzic, *Ilot de Er-Yoh, Houat, 1921-1925*. Vannes, 1930.

6   Giot, *Bull. Soc. Préhist. Fr.*, 49, 1952, p. 522, and 55, 1958, pp. 269 and 704.

7   Cogné and Giot, *Bull. Soc. Préhist. Fr.*, 49, 1952, p. 388; 50, 1953, p. 37; 51, 1954, p. 28, and 54, 1957, p. 240.

8   Cogné and Giot, *Bull. Soc. Préhist. Fr.*, 52, 1955. Giot, *ibid.*, 56, 1959, p. 43.

9   Le Rouzic, *Revue Archéologique*, 2, 1933, p. 189.

10 Gaillard, *Bull. Soc. Anthropologie Paris*, 3, 1892, p. 37.

11 *cf*. chapter III, note 8.

12 Martin, *Bull. et Mém. Soc. Emulation Côtes-du-Nord*, 38, 1900, p. 24

13 Daniel, *Proceedings Prehistoric Society*, 5, 1939, p. 143, has argued that these monuments are 'transepted Gallery Graves'.

14 L'Helgouach, *Travaux Laboratoire d'Anthropologie . . . Rennes*, 1956.

15 Du Châtellier, *Bull. et Mém. Soc. Emulation Côtes-du-Nord*, 21, 1883, p. 1.

16 L'Helgouach, *Congrès Préhistorique de France*, 15, 1956, p. 692.

17 Bénard, *cf*. Bibliography, 1929; L'Helgouach, *Annales de Bretagne*, 64, 1957, p. 1; Gaudron, *cf*. note 4; Collum, *The Tressé Iron-Age Megalithic Monument*, Oxford, 1935.

18 Giot, *Annales de Bretagne*, 66, 1959, p. 5.

CHAPTER VI

1   Old excavations, *cf. Bull. Soc. Polymathique Morbihan*, 1862, 1863 and 1864.

2   Le Rouzic, *cf.* Bibliography, 1932; *Bull. Soc. Polymathique Morbihan*, 1935, p. 6.

CHAPTER VII

1   Prof. R. de Valera has told us that in Ireland this technique is still in use.

2   Cariou, *Bull. Soc. Préhistorique Fr.*, 55, 1958, p. 444.

3   Du Châtellier, *Matériaux*, 17, 1881, p. 49.

4   Le Rouzic and M. and S. J. Péquart, *cf.* Bibliography, 1923; Marsille, *Bull. Soc. Polymathique Morbihan*, 1926, p. 180; L'Hostis, *Bull. Soc. Préhist. Fr.*, 30, 1933, p. 127.

5   Guénin, *cf.* Bibliography, 1936. G. Guénin had prepared a special study about the Breton menhirs, but it was never published.

6   Bachelot de La Pilaye described such earthworks in the Crozon district (Finistère).

7   Merlet, *Bull. Soc. Hist. et Arch de Bretagne*, 10, 1929, p. 13.

8   *cf.* Le Rouzic, Bibliography, 1930.

9   In the Carnac alignments, these stones which are definitely known to have been re-erected recently have a little square hole near their base, filled in with pink cement.

10 A valuable and precise enough description of the state of things before any restoration is to be found in: Blair and Ronalds, *Sketches at Carnac (Brittany) in 1834*; or, *Notes, etc.* London, 1836. All the other publications of that period are madly romantic. Just before the beginning of restorations one has: Miln, *Fouilles faites à Carnac (Bretagne)*, *Les Alignements de Kermario*, Rennes, 1881. The only recent and reliable description is that of: Schuchhardt, *Praehistorische Zeitschrift*, 32-33, 1941-42, p. 305. A precise plan of Kerlescan is given in: Hülle, *cf.* Bibliography, 1942.

11 Devoir, *Bull. Soc. Archéologique Finistère*, 38, 1911, p. 3.

12 The views of Gaillard, *L'Astronomie Préhistorique*, Paris, 1895, opened the way. The best work was that of Devoir, *cf.* note 11; *Mannus*, 1, 1909, p. 71; re-utilised by Bénard, *cf.* Bibliography, 1929.

The publications of Baudouin, Pény-Hirmenech and Baschmakoff are very wide of the mark.

The geographical school of Meynier tried in 1943-1945 to correlate the modern field orientations to the pre-historic system of Devoir.

13 Thus in the Côtes-du-Nord it has been thought that the giant menhirs of Kerguézennec, Bégard, of Pédernec, and of Pergat, Louargat, made a special system.

CHAPTER VIII

1 Piggott, *Proc. Prehist. Soc.*, 4, 1938, p. 52; 5, 1939, p. 193.

2 Cogné and Giot, *L'Anthropologie*, 55, 1951, p. 425. Briard and Giot, *Bull. Soc. Préhist. Fr.*, 53, 1956, p. 363. Briard and L'Helgouach, *cf.* Bibliography, 1957.

3 Briard and Maréchal, *Bull. Soc. Préhist. Fr.*, 55, 1958, p. 422.

4 Giot, *Bull. Soc. Arch. Finistère*, 80, 1954, p. 111; *Bull. Soc. Préhist. Fr.*, 53, 1956, p. 101.

5 Giot, *Congrès Préhistorique de France*, 15, 1956, p. 524.

6 Sandars, *Bronze Age Cultures in France*, Cambridge, 1957, argues (p. 59) that our 'series are specifically not divisions of chronology', a point of view that overlooks most facts.

7 Briard, *Bull. Soc. Préhist. Fr.*, 55, 1958, p. 20.

8 The 'jar' of Kerstrobel has even been attributed recently, by Sandars (*cf. l. c.*, note 6, p. 281), to the end of the Urnfield culture, in the Early Iron Age, or even Hallstatt B II, because she did not realise it came from a barrow! *cf. Bull. Soc. Préhist. Fr.*, 55, 1958, p. 46.

CHAPTER IX

1 For Morbihan, numerous papers by Marsille, *Bull. Soc. Polymathique du Morbihan*, 1913, 1932, 1937, 1938, etc.

2 Giot, *Bull. Soc. Arch. Finistère*, 75, 1949, p. 9. Briard, *Travaux Laboratoire d'Anthropologie ... de Rennes*, 1956 and 1958.

3 Latest reassessment by Savory, *Proc. Prehist. Soc.*, 14, 1948, p. 155. Briard, *Congrès Préhistorique de France*, 15, 1956, p. 313.

4 Prof. Kimmig no longer believes in the immediate Urnfield relationship between pots found in certain Passage Graves of the Morbihan district, Kermarquer, La-Trinité-sur-Mer, and Pendrec, Crach, in Iron Age contexts.

5 Du Breil de Pontbriand, *Bull. Soc. Hist. et Arch. Bretagne*, 14, 1933, p. 29; *Bull. et Mém. Soc. Emulation Côtes-du-Nord*, 64, 1932, p. 147, and 65, 1933, p. 163.

6 Giot, *Bull. Soc. Arch. Finistère*, 80, 1954, p. 55.

7 Fournier, Giot, L'Helgouach and Sieveking, *Bull. et Mém. Soc. Emulation Côtes-du-Nord*, 85, 1956, p. 10.

8 Champaud, *Annales de Bretagne*, 64, 1957, p. 46.

CHAPTER X

1 The chronology is that of Hatt, *Bull. Soc. Préhist. Fr.*, 51, 1954, p. 379, with the equivalences in the systems of Kimmig and Reinecke.

2 Marsille, *Bull. Soc. Polymathique Morbihan*, 1923, p. 3, 1924, p. 78; Le Rouzic, *ibid.*, 1933, p. 29.

3 *cf.* chapter IX, note 4.

4 Giot, *Annales de Bretagne*, 59, 1952, p. 211, with general bibliography.

5 Giot and Cogné, *Gallia*, 9, 1951, p. 1.

6 Couissin, *Revue Archéologique*, 1924, p. 292; Clarke and Hawkes, *Proc. Prehist. Soc.*, 21, 1955, p. 224.

7 Giot, Briard and L'Helgouach, *Annales de Bretagne*, 65, 1958, p. 15.

8 Wheeler and Richardson, *cf.* Bibliography, 1957.

9 Giot, *Annales de Bretagne*, 62, 1955, p. 202, and 65, 1958, p. 33.

10 Murray-Threipland, *Archaeological Journal*, 100, 1943, p. 128.

11 *cf.* chapter IX, note 8.

12 Merlet, *Mémoires Soc. Hist. et Arch. de Bretagne*, 30, 1950, p. 5, and 31, 1951, p. 137; Merlat, *Annales de Bretagne*, 59, 1952, p. 93.

13 Dr J. B. Colbert de Beaulieu kindly provided the information for this paragraph; his is the only detailed scientific work done on the Armorican coinage. Colbert de Beaulieu, *Revue belge de Numismatique*, 94, 1948; 96, 1950; 97, 1951; 99, 1953; 102, 1956; 103, 1957; *Mémoires Soc. Hist. et Arch. de Bretagne*, 33, 1953 and 34, 1954; *Annales de Bretagne*, 59, 1952; 60, 1953; 61, 1954; 62, 1955; 63, 1956; 64, 1957; 65, 1958; 66, 1959.

14 Denis, *Annales de Bretagne*, 61, 1954, p. 126; Merlat, *ibid.*, 61, 1954, p. 154; Creston, *ibid.*, 63, 1956, p. 88, and 65, 1958, p. 59; Emmanuelli, *ibid.*, 63, 1956, p. 55.

Bibliographical Guide

Books dealing with Breton prehistory are few. Besides those general works on French or European prehistory where the basic essentials are to be found in addition to much valuable specific information, the principal, reasonably up-to-date or useful books on Armorican antiquities are the following:

C. BENARD (Le Pontois), 'Le Finistère Préhistorique'. *Publications de l'Institut International d'Anthropologie*, III, 1929, Paris. Work to be used with extreme caution; numerous illustrations, but often with wrong captions.

J. BRIARD AND J. L'HELGOUACH, 'Chalcolithique, Néolithique Secondaire, Survivances néolithiques à l'Age du Bronze Ancien en Armorique'. *Travaux du Laboratoire d'Anthropologie de la Faculté des Sciences de Rennes*, 1957.

P. DU CHATELLIER, *La Poterie aux Epoques Préhistoriques et Gauloises en Armorique*. Rennes and Paris, 1897; *Les Epoques Préhistoriques et Gauloises dans le Finistère*. 2ème éd., Rennes and Quimper, 1907.

V. C. C. COLLUM, *The Tressé Iron-Age Megalithic Monument*. Oxford, 1935. *L'Allée couverte de Tressé*. Paris, 1938. To be used with extreme caution.

P. R. GIOT, 'Armoricains et Bretons, étude anthropologique'. *Travaux du Laboratoire d'Anthropologie de la Faculté des Sciences de Rennes*, 1951.

P. R. GIOT, J. L'HELGOUACH AND J. BRIARD, 'Menhirs et Dolmens, Monuments Mégalithiques de Bretagne'. *Images de Bretagne*, X, Châteaulin, 1957 and 1959.

G. GUENIN, *Pierres à légendes de Bretagne, le Folklore Préhistorique de la Bretagne*. Paris, 1936.

W. HÜLLE, 'Die Steine von Carnac'. *Führer zur Urgeschichte*, XV, Leipzig, 1942.

M. JACQ, *Catalogue du Musée Archéologique J. Miln—Z. Le Rouzic*. Carnac, 1942.

Z. LE ROUZIC, *Les Monuments Mégalithiques de Carnac et de Locmariaquer, leur destination, leur âge*. 10 editions, from 1897 to 1953, Carnac; *Les*

Cromlechs de Er-Lannic, Carnac, 1930; *Tumulus du Mont-St-Michel,* Carnac, 1932.

Z. LE ROUZIC, M. AND S. J. PEQUART, *Carnac, fouilles faites dans la région, campagne 1922.* Nancy, 1923.

L. MARSILLE, *Catalogue du Musée Archéologique de la Société Polymathique du Morbihan.* Vannes, 1921.

A. MILLON, *Pauvres Pierres! Les Mégalithes Bretons devant la Science.* Saint-Brieuc and Paris, 1911.

M. AND S. J. PEQUART, *Hoëdic, deuxième Station-Nécropole du Mésolithique côtier armoricain.* Anvers, 1954.

M. AND S. J. PEQUART, M. BOULE AND H. V. VALLOIS, 'Téviec, Station-Nécropole mésolithique du Morbihan'. *Archives de l'Institut de Paléontologie Humaine,* XVIII, Paris, 1937.

M. AND S. J. PEQUART AND Z. LE ROUZIC, *Corpus des Signes Gravés des Monuments Mégalithiques du Morbihan.* Paris, 1927.

Trésors Archéologiques de l'Armorique Occidentale. Société d'Emulation des Côtes-du-Nord, Saint-Brieuc, 1886.

R. E. M. WHEELER AND K. M. RICHARDSON, 'Hill-Forts of Northern France'. *Reports of the Research Committee of the Society of Antiquaries of London,* XIX, 1957.

The bulk of the information on Breton antiquities is distributed in nearly two thousand papers or notes published, in general periodicals but chiefly in regional ones. The basic bibliographical reference work is:

R. MONTANDON, *Bibliographie Génerale des Travaux Palethnologiques et Archéologiques,* France. III. Geneva, Lyon and Paris, 1926.—Premier Supplément du Tome III. Geneva, Lyon and Paris, 1928; continued by *Société Préhistorique Française,* Supplément à la Bibliographie Générale des Travaux Palethnologiques et Archéologiques. Paris, 1953 (*Bulletin de la Société Préhistorique Française,* XLIX, 1952). One can also consult with advantage:

Bibliographie Générale des Travaux Historiques et Archéologiques publiés par les Sociétés Savantes de la France. Paris, 1888 onwards.

J. COUPEL, *Bibliographie d'articles de périodiques concernant la Bretagne, 1793-1900.* Rennes, 1911; continued by 'Bibliographie Bretonne' in *Annales de Bretagne,* Rennes, 1901 onwards.

We wish to thank the Museum d'Histoire Naturelle of Toulouse for the photograph used in Plate 1; M. Jos Le Doaré, Châteaulin (Finistère), for photographs nos. 7, 8, 9, 10, 11, 12, 13, 30, 31, 32, 34, 35, 36, 37, 39, 40, 42, 43, 44, 45, 46, 47, 48, 49, 68; the Ashmolean Museum, Oxford, for nos. 17 and 50; M. Emile Le Stir, Ploudalmezeau (Finistère), for nos. 58 and 59; M. A. Cassan, Penmarch (Finistère), for no. 52; and M. L. Lengyel for nos. 72 and 73.

The line illustrations have all been re-drawn, often with modifications and corrections, at the Laboratoire d'Anthropologie, Faculté des Sciences, Rennes: fig. 2 after Dr. M. Gruet; plans 6, 7, 8, 20, 21, 22, after unpublished papers by Z. Le Rouzic; figs. 25 a and b, 26 a and c, 38 a and c, 51 a, 63, 64, after P. Du Châtellier; figs. 25 c and d, 33, 34, after A. Martin; 27 b after W. C. Lukis; 38 b after J. M. Abgrall; figs. 41, 44, 48, 49 after the album of *Trésors archéologiques*; 56 after L. Marsille; 66 inspired by R. E. M. Wheeler; 68 inspired by R. Y. Creston.

1

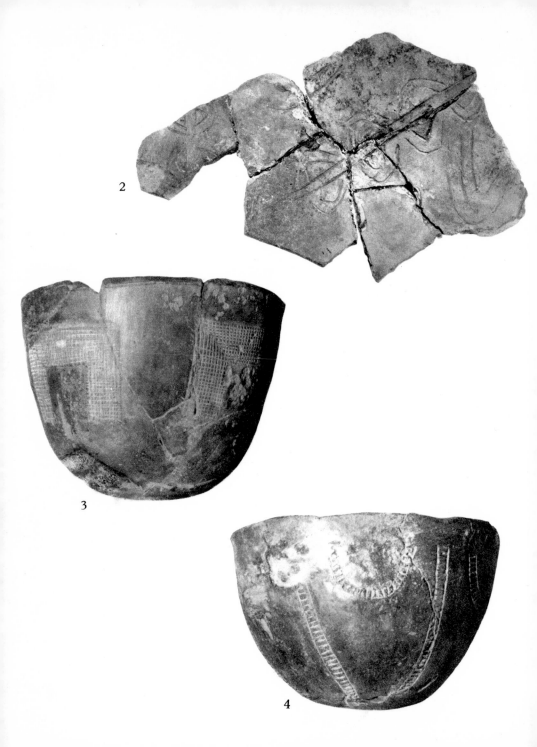

2

3

4

6

7

8

9

11

12

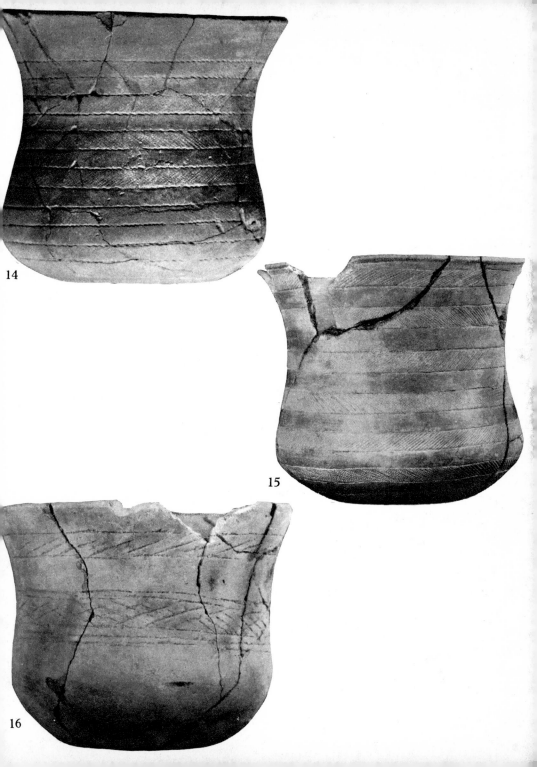

14

15

16

17

18

19

20

25

26

27

28

29

31

32

33

34

35

36

37

40

41

42

44

46

48

49

50

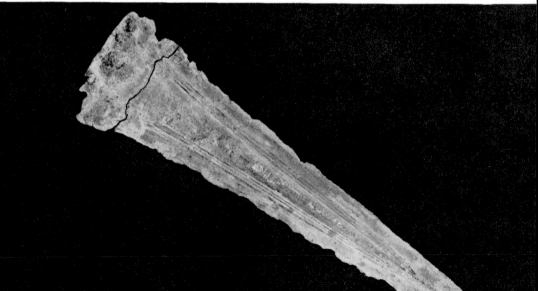

51

52

53

54

55

56

57

58

59

60

61

62

63

64   65

66   67

70

71

a

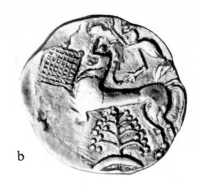

b

c

d

e

f

a

b

c

d

e

f

Notes on the Plates

1 Reconstruction of a Mesolithic double grave in the cemetery of Téviec, Saint-Pierre-Quiberon (M.), with antler garland. The bodies were adorned with shell necklaces. Muséum d'Histoire Naturelle, Toulouse.

2 Fragment of a Neolithic pot with channelled decoration, from the long mound of Mané-Hui, Carnac (M.). Actual size. Musée Miln.

3 Neolithic pot decorated with incised checkered pattern, from the Passage Grave of Er-Mar, Crach (M.). Height 54 mm. Musée des Antiquités Nationales.

4 Neolithic pot decorated with incised festoons, from the Passage Grave of Park-Néhué, Riantec (M.). Height 52 mm. Musée des Antiquités Nationales.

5 Sectional view of the chamber, Passage Grave C of the large cairn at Barnenez, Plouézoc'h (F.); the corbelled vault is clearly visible in this ruined monument (internal height 4 metres).

6 The corbelled roof (seen from below) of the chamber of Passage Grave G[1] in the large cairn at Barnenez, Plouézoc'h (F.).

7 Passage Grave of Kermané, Saint-Philibert (M.).

8 Group of Passage Graves at Kerran, Locmariaquer (M.).

9 Two of the three Passage Graves at Mané-Kerioned, Carnac (M.).

10 Passage Grave of Keroch, Saint-Philibert (M.).

11 Engravings of axes or adzes with hafts, on an orthostat in the chamber of the Mané-Kerioned Passage Grave, Carnac (M.).

12 Engraving of a hafted axe beneath the capstone covering the 'Table des Marchands' Passage Grave, Locmariaquer (M.).

13 End orthostat of the 'Table des Marchands' Passage Grave, Locmariaquer (M.). Ogival in shape, it has a shield on its front face, decorated with rows of 'crooks' on either side of the vertical axis, and with 'streamers' around the outside.

P

14 Bell Beaker, decorated with bands outlined with cord impressions and filled in with comb patterns, from the Gallery Grave of Men-ar-Rompet, Kerbors (C.-du-N.). Height 130 mm. Laboratoire d'Anthropologie de la Faculté des Sciences, Rennes.

15 Bell Beaker with comb pattern, from the Gallery Grave of Men-ar- Rompet, Kerbors (C.-du-N.), decorated with white incrustations. Height 152 mm. Laboratoire d'Anthropologie de la Faculté des Sciences, Rennes.

16 Bell Beaker with badly imprinted comb decoration, from the Gallery Grave of Men-ar-Rompet, Kerbors (C.-du-N.). Height 121 mm. Laboratoire d'Anthropologie de la Faculté des Sciences, Rennes.

17 Late Neolithic vessel, flower-pot type, from the angled Passage Grave of Run-Aour, Plomeur. Height 110 mm. Musée Préhistorique Finistérien.

18 Late Neolithic carinated bowl, from the Passage Grave of Crugou, Plovan (F.). Musée des Antiquités Nationales.

19 Late Neolithic pot, decorated with crude channelling, from one of the Passage Graves of the Butten-er-Hah cairn, Ile-de-Groix (M.). Musée des Antiquités Nationales.

20 Late Neolithic pot decorated with crude channelling, from the Passage Grave of Conguel, Quiberon (M.). Height 85 mm. Musée des Antiquités Nationales.

21 Late Neolithic pot, decorated with crude channelling, from the Passage Grave of Conguel, Quiberon (M.). Height 115 mm. Musée des Antiquités Nationales.

22 Carinated bowl from the Gallery Grave of Men-ar-Rompet, Kerbors (C.-du-N.). Height 123 mm. Laboratoire d'Anthropologie de la Faculté des Sciences, Rennes.

23 Late Neolithic pot, so-called 'collared flask', from the Passage Grave of Lann-Blaën, Guidel (M.). Height 160 mm. Musée des Antiquités Nationales.

24 Late Neolithic pot, so-called 'collared flask', from the Gallery Grave of Mélus, Ploubazlanec (C.-du-N.). Height 135 mm. Musée des Antiquités Nationales.

25 Flat axes with splayed cutting edge and flat-tanged dagger (Palmella point type) of copper alloy, dredged from the Loire at Trentemoult, near Nantes, and (centre, vertically placed) dagger or halberd with cylindrical base and pronounced median rib, dredged from the Loire at Paimboeuf (L.-A.). Length of dagger, 205 mm. Musée Départemental, Nantes.

26 Polished Finistère axes, of fibrolite, of flint with flat sides, of dolerite, and button type axe of dolerite. Lengths 205, 158, 169 and 180 mm. respectively. Musée Préhistorique Finistérien.

27 Boat-shaped battle-axe of hornblendite from a cist at Mané-Meur, Quiberon (M.). Length 153 mm. Musée Miln.

28 Dagger of Grand-Pressigny flint from the angled Passage Grave of Mané-er-Loh, Locoal-Mendon (M.). Length 174 mm. Musée Miln.

29 Dagger of Grand-Pressigny flint from near the Saint-Michel barrow, Carnac (M.). Length 140 mm. Musée Miln.

30 Engraving on one of the orthostats of the angled Passage Grave of Pierres-Plates, Locmariaquer (M.).

31 Engraving on one of the orthostats of the angled Passage Grave of Luffang, Crach (M.). Musée Miln.

32 The Roche-aux-Fées, a megalithic structure of the Loire type, at Essé (I.-et-V.).

33 Gallery Grave of Men-ar-Rompet, Kerbors (C.-du-N.). Length 7 m. 50.

34 Gallery Grave of Kergüntuil, Trégastel (C.-du-N.). Length 22 m.

35 Gallery Grave of Mougau-Bihan, Commana (F.). Length 13 m.

36 Mound at Tumiac, Arzon (M.). Height 15 m., diameter 55 m. Carnac group.

37 *Arc-bouté* Gallery Grave of Goulet-Riec, Riec-sur-Belon (F.).

38 *Arc-bouté* Gallery Grave of Castel-Ruffel, Saint Goazec (F.).

39, 40 Engravings of Gavrinis Passage Grave, Larmor-Baden (M.). Concentric half circles, looking like finger-prints (39), axes and serpents (40).

41 Polished axe of translucent jadeite, with a perforation for suspension, found at Kerham, Ploëmeur (M.). Length 157 mm. Musée Miln.

42 Menhir of Kerloas, Plouarzel (F.). Height 12 metres.

43 Menhir of Kerampeulven, Berrien (F.). Height 5 m.

44 Christianised menhir of Men-Marz, Brignogan (F.). Height 8 m.

45 Christianised menhir of Saint-Duzec, Pleumeur-Bodou (C.-du-N.) on which the Instruments of the Passion were carved around 1674. Height 8 m.

46 Alignments of Ménec at Carnac (M.).

47 Alignments of Ménec at Carnac (M.).

48 Alignments of Kermario at Carnac (M.).

49 Alignment of Lagatjar at Camaret (F.).

50 Material from the barrow of Saint-Fiacre, Melrand (M,): two axes with small flanges; six triangular daggers, damaged in varying degrees; a dagger with a pronounced rib; a dagger with a metal hilt (of an unusual type for this region); two metal arrowheads, also unusual; a rectangular amber spacing bead, from a crescent-shaped necklace. Length of the largest axe, 180 mm. Ashmolean Museum, Oxford.

51 Triangular dagger from a barrow at Kervellerin, Cléguer (M.). Length 280 mm. Musée Miln.

52 Biconical pot with four handles from the barrow of Kersaint-Plabennec (F.). Height 260 mm. Musée Préhistorique Finistérien.

53 Biconical pot with one handle, decorated, from the barrow of Run-Mellou-Poaz, Spézet (F.). Height 240 mm. Musée des Antiquités Nationales.

54 Biconical pot with two handles, decorated, from the barrow of Menez-Pengoanez, Loqueffret (F.). Height 162 mm. Musée Préhistorique Finistérien.

55 Decorated pot with one handle from the barrow of Kervern, Plozévet (F.). Height 200 mm. Musée des Antiquités Nationales.

56 Decorated biconical pot with three handles from the barrow of Lannilis (F.). Height 183 mm. Musée Préhistorique Finistérien.

57 Decorated biconical pot with one handle from a barrow at Kergoz, Plounévez-Loc'hrist (F.). Height 120 mm. Musée Préhistorique Finistérien.

58, 59 Decorated one-handled pot, from a barrow at Park-Roz, Plourin-Ploudalmezeau (F.). Height 110 mm. (59 shows the base). Private collection.

60 Cinerary urn from the circular grave at Boquidet, Sérent (M.). Height 212 mm. Musée Miln.

61 Cinerary urn from the circular grave of Nignol, Carnac (M.). Height 230 mm. Musée Miln.

62 Cinerary urn from the circular grave of Nignol, Carnac (M.). Height 300 mm. Musée Miln.

63 Cinerary urn with pedestal, decorated with nipples on the body, from the barrow of Lannvréon, Peumerit (F.). Height 300 mm. Musée Préhistorique Finistérien.

64 Cinerary urn from the cemetery of Kerviltré, Saint-Jean-Trolimon (F.). Height 235 mm. Musée Préhistorique Finistérien.

65 Cinerary urn from the cemetery of Roz-an-Trémen, Plomeur (F.). Height 260 mm. Musée Préhistorique Finistérien.

66 Cinerary urn with pedestal and decoration, from Tronoan, Saint-Jean-Trolimon (F.). Height 163 mm. Musée Préhistorique Finistérien.

67 Cinerary urn from Guissény (F.). Height 232 mm. Musée Préhistorique Finistérien.

68 Christianised quadrangular stela of Kroas-Teo, Locmaria-Plouzané (F.). Height 3 m. 60.

69 Statue with raised thumbs from Lanneunoc, Plounévez-Loc'hrist (F.). Height 600 mm. Musée Préhistorique Finistérien.

70 Cliff castle, Pointe de Lostmarc'h, Crozon (F.). A double rampart is visible. Seen from the W.

71 Cliff castle, Pointe de Kastel-Meur. Cléden-Cap-Sizun (F.). Three ramparts and hut-platforms are visible. Seen from the S.W.

72 (a) Very early gold stater of the Veneti. Obverse. Diameter 20 mm. Bibliothèque Nationale.
(b) Very early Armorican stater, gold. Reverse. Diameter 22 mm. Private collection.
(c) Early stater of the Veneti, pale gold. Reverse. Diameter 22 mm. Private collection.
(d) Stater of the Veneti, alloy, found in the hoard at Pipriac (I.-et-V.). Obverse. Diameter 23 mm. Musée de Rennes.
(e) Reverse of the coin shown under (d).
(f) Stater of the Veneti, alloy, found in the hoard at Pipriac (I.-et-V.). Reverse. Diameter 22 mm. Musée de Rennes.

73 (a) Stater of the Osismi, black gold. Obverse. Diameter 23 mm. Bibliothèque Nationale.
(b) Gold stater of the Osismi. Reverse. Diameter approx. 23 mm. Bibliothèque Nationale.
(c) Gold stater of the Namnetes. Obverse. Diameter 24 mm. Bibliothèque Nationale.
(d) Stater of the Coriosolitae, alloy. Obverse. Diameter 22 mm. Bibliothèque Nationale.
(e) Stater of the Coriosolitae, alloy. Reverse. Diameter 22 mm. Bibliothèque Nationale.
(f) Stater of the Redones, alloy. Reverse. Diameter 22 mm. Bibliothèque Nationale.

Index